DATE DUE			
JUN 2 8 2007			
Swift			
ILL			
to: (20B			
11-26-08			
GAYLORD			PRINTED IN U.S.A

A Zuni Life

A Pueblo Indian in Two Worlds

Virgil Wyaco

Transcribed and edited by J. A. Jones
Historical Sketch by Carroll L. Riley

❖

University of New Mexico Press
Albuquerque

✚ *For Laura and my children*

Library of Congress Cataloging-in-Publication Data

Wyaco, Virgil, 1926–
A Zuni life: a Pueblo Indian in two worlds / Virgil Wyaco; transcribed
and edited by J.A. Jones; historical sketch by Carroll L. Riley.—1st ed.

p. cm.

Includes bibliographical references.

ISBN 0–8263–1880–0 (cloth)—ISBN 0–8263–1881–9 (paper)

  1. Wyaco, Virgil, 1926– .
  2. Zuni Indians—Biography.
  I. Jones, J. A. (John Alan), 1923– .
  II. Riley, Carroll L.
  III. Title.

E99.Z9W93 1998
973'.04979—dc21 97–35058
CIP

CONTENTS

*T*his book had its genesis in the period just after World War II when three returning veterans decided, for varying reasons, to enroll at the University of New Mexico. All three had been in the European Theatre during the war but met for the first time at the university. Jay Jones and Carroll Riley enrolled as undergraduates in the anthropology program while Virgil Wyaco, an undergraduate in engineering, worked with departmental anthropologists who were studying the Zuni language. The three young ex-soldiers were roommates for a time and saw a great deal of each other socially. Each visited Zuni Pueblo, Virgil for obvious reasons, and Jones and Riley because they were studying Pueblo culture, history, and prehistory.

In the years that followed, Jones and Riley became professional anthropologists, going into different subfields of that profession. Jones developed a strong interest in psychological anthropology but eventually drifted out of the field to become a successful novelist under the name Courtway Jones. Riley continued studying the ethnohistory and archaeology of the Southwest, authoring several books on the subject, though he also maintained a research interest in Latin America and in Europe. Wyaco's career subsequent to his college years is told in the autobiographical section of this book. The three men remained friends, and even though living in different parts of the country, they saw a fair amount of each other.

For years the three had talked, more or less seriously, about collaborating on a life of Virgil Wyaco. Eventually Jones and Riley retired to Las Vegas, New Mexico, and Virgil settled in Zuni itself. By the beginning of the 1990s the plans for a book were beginning to take firm shape. In 1992 the three applied for and received a grant from the New Mexico Endowment for the Humanities to put Wyaco's autobiography on tape. Riley served as project director, and Virgil Wyaco fulfilled the Endowment's lecture requirement by giving a well-received public lecture in January 1993 in Las Vegas.

The project strategy was for Wyaco to make audio tapes of his life story, starting with his early life and schooling. There would be considerable emphasis on Virgil's experiences in World War II and then a major treatment of his postwar experiences back in the Southwest. Once these tapes were transcribed, the three authors went over the manuscript, editing, annotating, collating, filling in gaps, and checking for accuracy. It was also necessary to make sure that discussions of Zuni religious and ceremonial life did not involve sensitive esoteric religious data.

Courtway Jones, because of his novelistic skills, was then given the task of rephrasing the story into a consistent and readable style, while Riley, the southwestern expert, undertook the writing of a short history of the Zuni people. Once these drafts had been rewritten, Virgil Wyaco and his wife Laura read both the autobiography and the history and gave final approval.

CHAPTER I

*I*t snowed the night I was born, a soft fall that covered the muddy ground and would melt into the earth to awaken the seeds in the spring.

You're frowning. You Whites hear the word "snow" and think of slippery streets; you hear the word "rain" and think of canceled golf dates. It's not like that with the Zuni. Another Zuni or a Hopi would know what I'm saying; maybe even a Navajo. You have to listen to my words. I want to tell you the story of my life so it can be written down for young Zuni to read, but you have to listen. First, you have to understand about rain.

Rain is brought to us by the *koko*. You think of them as *katcina*, like the ones in the shops in Santa Fe, but katcina is not a Zuni word. We call them koko. The koko are our ancestors, even the first koko. Back then the world was soft and the Zuni climbed out of the underworld and crossed the first stream, some of our children turned into frogs. They swam all the way to the sacred lake, Kothluwalawa. They were lost to us, but they didn't die. They grew up to be the koko and danced under water on the bottom of the lake; it's like a dance hall down there. We Zuni believe we will become koko when we die.

It is always "now" where the koko are; they don't feel the passing of time as we do. They don't even think of the seasons unless we remind them. It's hard for them to hear us, for their minds are filled with nothing but dancing. But when all the Zuni dance together, they shake the earth and the koko can feel it, even in Kothluwalawa. Then they bring the clouds to us and we know our loved ones, our fathers and mothers and even our children who have died, have come to help us. The gift of rain they bring is like a blessing. Snow is like a promise.

You can read in the anthropological reports of Cushing and Stevenson and Bunzel about our prayers for rain. We have no secrets left. You Whites have stolen them all. When you read there that we pray to our mothers, the clouds, you probably think it's just symbolic. It's not.

Do you understand? When I say, "It snowed all through the night I was born," I mean the koko were aware of me. It was a blessing. They were saying, "We know this one, this young Zuni. We will bring him rain. He will have plenty to eat. He will have a good life." My own mother became one with the koko when I was about three. I remember when my father took me to see the Shalako for the first time. It must have been shortly before my mother died. I was frightened at first, for they wear masks of monsters and I cried. My father took me on his lap and calmed me, saying they would not hurt me. Someone must have told me my mother went to join the koko after she died, for I have always loved the koko since I was a child. At Shalako time the gods, the koko, come from the four corners of the earth to renew their ties with the Zuni. Even now, I think of my mother as with them, invisible, but aware of me. My aunts told me stories about her and the times we had together, so often I can't be sure which are my memories and which are theirs. They said she laughed all the time. She had everything. She was pretty and had nice clothes. Her father was the richest man in Zuni. Her husband was the best looking; all the other women wanted to marry him. Someone was so envious that her spite reached out and made my mother sick. That's what witches do. It's unlucky to have too much. Even if you're generous, there are some things you can't give away.

There have always been witches. Our sacred stories of the emergence of the Zuni from the underworlds speak of it. You anthropologists call our accounts of the first times "origin myths," and wonder how an educated man like me can believe in them. I wonder why many Whites insist that God made the earth and all the creatures that inhabit it in six days. I am amazed that educated men want to teach "creationism" to my grandchildren in school as an alternative to evolutionary theory. I've been told it's because what Indians believe is merely superstition and what Whites believe is revealed religion. I'm not convinced of the truth of that!

Maybe our myths are closer to evolutionary theory because Indians are nearer to nature, as I have been told. Our myths, then, speak of four underworlds, the first one of total darkness, where we could not see one another and stepped on each others' toes. The second was a water moss world, which was still dark. The third was a mud world. Only when we reached the fourth world was there even the faintest light. We called that one "wing world" because the rays of sunlight were like birds' wings.

When we finally climbed to the surface of the earth it was still soft, and we found we had tails and webbed hands and feet. Maybe you see why we find evolutionary theory easier to believe than your Bible.

Of course, your Bible is written and our sacred history is merely related word-for-word by men whose lives have been devoted to learning it and telling it without alteration. But then, the Zuni do not remember every single thing. If they did, it would take four years to relate the story rather than merely four winter nights.

The old men say that gods led us from the underworlds, and cut off our tails and split our webs with stone knifes so we become as we are now. At first, we were wanderers rather than farmers. Not all the Zuni were strong enough to struggle to the surface world in the first wave of emergence. The last to come out were a man and a woman dressed in coarse woven hoods that moved in the wind. They were witches.

"Where are you going?" they asked us.

"To seek the Middle Place," we answered.

"We want to go with you to the Middle Place."

"We do not want you with us."

"We will destroy the earth," they said. "We have all the seeds."

"What do you want?" the god who led us asked.

"We want two of your children," the witches replied.

"What will you do with them?"

"We will kill them to bring the rain. Our gift of seeds will not grow unless there is much rain."

And the god said, "It is well."

So the god gave the witches his son and his daughter, and when they went to sleep the witches touched them and shot poison into their hearts so they died. The witches buried them and it rained heavily for four days. On the fifth day, the boy rose from the earth, alive. It rained four more days and the girl arose. That night, the witches planted all the seeds.

The next day, the corn and squash and melons were sprout-
ing from the earth. Of course, nothing that comes from
witches is good by itself. Other creatures helped make the
food nutritious to men, but the witches started it. Because
the god promised in our name that they could come with us,
they have been among us always. I've heard it suggested that
the sacrifice of the god's children and their subsequent res-
urrection to bring the Zuni food crops sounds like a diffu-
sion from western culture. It is said we added this part of
the story to our account of the emergence, envious of the
story of the son of your god, as written in your Bible. It's
said with condescension that ours is merely an oral tradition, and your story rests on written history. Does it really?
Have you any writings of Jesus, himself? Have you any writings by anyone who knew him personally and heard him
speak? No, you don't. Even today there is argument over
how much of your Bible is authentic and how much based
on documents that originated in the first and second century. At best, it would seem to me, these documents were
based on oral traditions, like ours. Maybe it's just that
Whites can't believe that our god and your god might be the
same. And maybe it's unthinkable that if he were sacrificed
once for Whites, he could be sacrificed again for Indians.
We do not know why the witches were entrusted with
seeds, but our holy men talk about such things. It has been
suggested that if no one ever died, the earth would become
overpopulated. Our death rates have always been higher
than yours. Death does not mean the same to us as it does to
you Whites. We mourn those who pass, as you do, but we
do not feel as much separated from our dead. On the long
ribbon that runs for each person, we are attached both to
the future and to the past. Ordinarily, we don't welcome

death, but we don't fear it. And we know that witches and death are related and have been since those first days.

There is no way to protect ourselves against witches completely. We Zuni make ourselves as strong as we can by thinking good thoughts. We are most vulnerable when we are young and weak or old and feeble, or merely asleep, as were the children of the god when the witches killed them. No matter how pure a man's thoughts are, he will die eventually. The most holy man in Zuni died recently in his nineties.

We know there are no accidents witches do not arrange, no illnesses they do not wish to happen. I was kicked by a horse once and broke three ribs. It was my fault for tickling the horse's stomach, but I'd done that before. Why did she kick me that once?

There are occasions when everyone is more vulnerable to the attacks of witches than usual, times when we are closest to the spirit world. Then everything must be done ritually, as we were taught by our ancestors. Anthropologists call these rituals "crisis rites." Birth is such a time. When I was born, my mother had women from her clan around to guard her and help with the birth. Old Woman Wabena, her own mother's sister, was the first to touch me as I came from the womb. She claimed me for her husband's kiva group to let the witches know I was protected. It was always done that way. There was rivalry among the midwives about who would be the first to touch the newborn child, but the idea was to protect it.

I was dried with corn meal, not a towel or rag. For the Zuni, corn meal is like what holy water is to Catholics. After I was dried, Old Woman Wabena cut and tied the

cord, wrapped me in a new blanket, and laid me in the little
cradle that had been prepared. An ear of corn was placed
beside me to protect me from any evil that might come
close to me for the next four days. It was almost like a vacci-
nation; it would help protect me the rest of my life. And
four is the Zuni sacred number. At the end of the four days
the corn was shelled and saved to plant, along with other
seeds, so I would grow as the corn grew.

My mother had to follow ritual, too, for she was as vulnerable as I. Many Zuni women have died in childbirth. Her
female relatives heated lava rocks in the fireplace and buried
them in a bed of sand for her to lie on. They changed the
rocks every morning and evening to keep her warm. Of
course, she laid on a blanket so she wouldn't get burned, but
she wasn't allowed to get up except to relieve and clean herself. She had to eat special food: nothing with salt was given
her. We were both watched through the first four days.
Even now, if a mother and child live through the first four
days, they should be all right for a while.

After my umbilical cord dried and fell off, it was buried
in the dirt floor of the house to keep it from falling into the
hands of witches. Cedar ashes taken from the hearth were
made into a paste and rubbed all over my body. Everything
about the cedar had medical value, the leaves, the bark, the
ashes. The cedar ashes paste would prevent me from having
body hair, would keep my skin as smooth as when I was
born. Even today I have very little body hair. The hearth itself is sacred, close to the spirit world. Before we eat we
take some of our food and offer it to the fire taken from the
hearth with a prayer to feed the ancestors. Ashes are clean,
free from anything evil.

You know the Navajo are afraid of dead people and avoid

hospitals because they are full of ghosts. They think the spirits of the dead are evil, like witches. We Zuni don't believe that. In the old days the Zuni died at home; our houses would be full of ghosts if we thought as the Navajo do. The spirit world is near when someone dies, but that is good. As with birth, the Zuni surround death with ritual, and acknowledge that it is as natural as life.

I don't remember my mother's funeral, but for the Zuni, they're all the same. Her aunts and sisters have told me about it. They washed and dressed her in a black manta and other hand-made clothing, something she could wear in Kothluwalawa. They put jewelry on her like she was going to dance, and by our reckoning, she was. People are no longer buried with their jewelry and other personal belongings. I think it's too bad. What will they wear in Kothluwalawa?

My little brother was still nursing when my mother died. He was only about a year old. The two of us went to live with her sister and her husband, and we learned to call them mother and father. They were happy to have us. Children are a blessing. What is hard to explain to Whites is that when we lost our mother, we lost our father, too. Children among the Zuni belong to the mother's family. There is never any question of custody when a family is broken up by death or divorce. My real father continued to take an interest in me, giving my aunt money for clothes when he had it, but mostly my brother and I grew up ragged. My father was always important to me, but my aunt and uncle were my "family." That's the way it is in Zuni.

CHAPTER 2

*M*y mother called me "Bacho." The word doesn't mean anything in Zuni. I've thought perhaps she meant to say "macho," the Spanish word for manly, for I'm told by my aunts that I was fearless as a child. The sounds "b" and "m" are much alike to Zuni ears. My aunts use the Zuni word, "meshiko," to describe my behavior then, which is closer in meaning to the English word "naughty" than manly. Perhaps I was both.

It wasn't just that I was indulged as a child in deference to my orphaned state, for I've been told I was the same before my mother died. One story that was a favorite of my aunt's, was the time I watched her and my mother resurface the kitchen floor. We had dirt floors then in our stone-walled houses and they wore out from traffic and spilled liquids. The surfaces were renewed much the same way that inside walls are plastered, by smoothing on a mixture of soft mud and straw by hand.

Evidently, after the renewed floor had dried and hardened I took the occasion of their absence to attempt to emulate their work. I used lard, rather than mud, however, and had smeared on half a can before they found me at work. The story always evokes laughter, though everyone has heard it many times. I laugh with everyone else. It is a good story if only because it is a source of laughter, for laughter is evidence of a good heart, one that is not troubled with witch feelings. One is apt to hear the same jokes again and again among the Zuni.

One of the stereotypes that Whites hold of Indians is that they are all stony faced and grim. Over time, perhaps, there has been little to laugh about in our face-to-face dealings with Whites, but among ourselves we laugh all the time. Teasing is constant and often sexual in nature, except with those persons to whom our culture requires that we show respect. With friends, there are few limits.

I've wondered since what effect the lard had, but I've never asked. It wasn't the point of the story. Asking a question like that would only cause anxiety; perhaps I would not hear the story again. There is a mutual understanding that laughter is appropriate, but not questions. Even gentle questions are considered aggressive.

I fear that I always did the opposite of what I was told to do by my parents. The contrary behavior I exhibited was amusing just because I was a child. Children are not expected to know better and though there is much verbal correction, it is not harsh. Children are never hit.

In the world outside of Zuni aggressive behavior is the mark of a confident man; a hearty grip accompanied by staring into another's eyes is proof of an open and honest nature. Being aggressive in this way is still one of the things I find hardest to do. When Indians shake hands, they don't squeeze, they merely touch flesh. Staring at another's face is insulting, a deliberate provocation. I have never tried to explain this to a White person. I have never found it necessary to explain it to another Indian. We Indians have few customs in common, but that one seems to be universal.

Pointing? Ah, yes. Pointing makes me so uncomfortable, I don't even like to think of it. I remember when I was first in school: I was little and scrawny and the teacher pointed at us because she didn't know anyone's name. It terrified me. Me, the one they called Bacho! I told my mother and she said that Whites didn't understand that pointing was witch behavior. You can still see old women, in the grocery store, pointing with a jerk of their head and a pursing of their lips to the big cans of peaches on the shelf behind the store-keeper, all the while fumbling with their pocketbooks clutched under their shawls. That's an accepted way for an Indian to point. Finger pointing is what witches do when they shoot poison into you. Whites seem to do it all the time.

Yes, when I was a very young child I was small and puny. I don't know why. I've heard psychologists call the condition a "failure to thrive," as if it were a cause and not a description. I do know I was not starved. No one had any money during the Depression, when I was young, but at least my family had enough to eat. My grandfather was reckoned to be the richest man in the pueblo because of his large sheep herd. We always had meat at our evening meal, mutton. Some folks in Zuni must have been hungry all the time back then.

While there was enough food, adequate clothing was an-other thing. I remember never feeling warm. The winters were often bitterly cold. We had only the fireplace for heat and for light at night, and customarily ate from a common bowl, sitting on the floor before the fire. No one had tables and chairs, or individual dishes, then. Since we had nothing to compare our lives with, we didn't feel our poverty. None-theless, I didn't thrive, and my aunt, whom I learned to call mother after my real mother's death, worried about me all the time, particularly because my little brother was so healthy.

In old Zuni, brothers and sisters looked after the younger ones. Mothers were mostly concerned with babies who were still nursing and with food preparation. And keeping children clean took an enormous amount of time and effort. Just think . . . all the water had to be hauled bucket by bucket to the house and heated for baths and laundry. I remember my brother Lee's diapers were made of flour sacks and had to be washed by hand. If there weren't a core of related females in every household, it would have been impossible to get everything done. It was my job to look after my little brother, Lee.

As soon as he could walk well enough to tag after me, Lee went with me everywhere. In the winter, up until the time I started school, it didn't matter, because I never went anyplace. In the summertime, though, I was forever having to wait for him to catch up. My friends all had little brothers, too, so I never felt unfairly burdened. When I turned six and had to go to school, I think the separation was harder on Lee than school was on me.

It must have been like caging a wild animal to put me in school. I might have been undersized, but I was tough. I hadn't even worn moccasins all summer long and the skin on my feet was so calloused I could walk through tumbleweeds and not even feel the stickers. My foster mother made me shirts and pants, and the government school issued us shoes, socks, and underwear, as well as shirts and pants for those kids who didn't have them.

Going to school for the first time was treated as a ritual. I was bathed, and my hair was cut to comply with the school regulations. My aunts untangled my hair with a fine-tooth comb to inspect my scalp for lice. When I was young, if we got head lice our mothers washed our hair with kerosene;

we called it coal oil back then. It stunk, but it worked.
Probably the lice couldn't stand the smell.

I didn't know a word of English when I entered first grade. Communication was difficult, for the teachers made no effort to learn Zuni; the effort was supposed to be all on our part. Even my given name was changed, from Bacho to Virgil, because that was the closest the enrolling clerk could come to the sound. I've been Virgil ever since; I don't suppose there's more than half a dozen people in Zuni who remember I used to be called Bacho.

After two months I was taken out of the Zuni day school and sent to the boarding school at Black Rock because I looked so sickly. Black Rock is a small town four miles east of Zuni, but still on the Reservation. That was hard, being away from my family. If I wasn't tough, I'd have died there. That was the worst winter we ever had. The snow was three feet deep. The fire in the wood stoves the Indian Service used to warm the dormitories burned out before morning, and I couldn't sleep because of the cold. I hated the food; it wasn't what I'd been used to. Looking back, no one should have to get used to food like that. I ate better in the army. At home we ate mostly mutton stew, pinto beans, cornmeal, roasted corn and fruit in season, and homemade wheat flour bread or tortillas cooked on top of the wood stove. We had green chile with every meal. A school nurse told my foster mother that a corn, beans, chili diet was as near a balanced one as anyone ate anywhere. The rest was just extra. My friend Cal Riley tells me that isn't exactly true. You need fat to metabolize the protein in the beans.

My grandfather raised wheat and had it ground into flour at the mill in Black Rock. Except in winter, when it was too cold to work outside, my aunts made bread in the *hor-*

nos, the beehive-shaped stone-and-mud ovens outside in the yard, maybe thirty loaves at a time. They stored the bread we used for our daily meals in barrels and it never got moldy. That's one thing that hasn't changed. We've added butter and milk and eggs to our diet, but most Zuni families still like to eat Indian food better than what you buy in the stores.

After a summer at home I hated to go back to the Black Rock school for second grade. My real father had a Bureau of Indian Affairs job at Black Rock, so I lived with him and went to the public school instead of the boarding school. He'd married Janice Wyaco's mother, so it wasn't too bad. Janice? Janice is my sister.

The school was near Dowa Yalanne, Corn Mountain, and my grandfather had a peach orchard not far from there. Sometimes I'd walk over to the orchard and bring a sack of fruit back to school. I got tired of the big kids beating up on me and my friends and taking the fruit away, so I complained to my uncle. I was still fearful of White adults; I couldn't tell them. My uncle must have gone to the school authorities for they put a stop to it.

All the children of the Bureau of Indian Affairs employees went to the Black Rock school. There was only one other Zuni family working for the Bureau, so we all talked English on the playground. I learned more English there than in the classroom. Our playground language was neither polite nor grammatical, but I gained a fluency then that has been useful ever since.

I went home again for the summer and was reunited with Lee and my aunts. Later, my father lost his job with the Bureau of Indian Affairs and could no longer afford to pay our school tuition, so I stayed home and was re-enrolled in the

free Zuni day school. At Zuni, we ate lunch at home, real
Indian food. I liked it better than Black Rock.

By the time I got to the third grade, I had grown stronger.
My foster mother had me chop kindling and haul water
from the pump to the house every afternoon after school.
She worked hard, herself. She started a garden and grew
chile, onions, spinach, cabbage, carrots, and tomatoes. Our
diet improved, but our clothes remained ragged. If the
school hadn't given us longjohns, we wouldn't have worn
any underwear. There was no money in Zuni to buy anything back then. Mostly, if you couldn't make it or grow it,
you went without. We did get kerosine lamps, so there was
light in the evening to do our school work. I could have
done without that improvement.

The school put up showers for the students but didn't
heat the bathhouse. We used to go to the school before it
opened and take showers, but our hair would freeze in the
wintertime before we reached home, a hundred yards away.
It's a wonder we didn't die from exposure.

When I completed the third grade, my foster mother's
husband, Vicenti, took me to the family sheep camp for the
summer. My grandfather had a thousand sheep and my foster father, my uncles, and a cousin were the shepherds. I
don't suppose I did much useful work, being that young, but
it was a start. I was there about two months and remember
a fierce electrical storm that seemed much closer and more
dangerous that any storm I'd known before down in Zuni.
We had only a canvas tent for protection. When I got back
home, I was dirty and bushy haired; my foster mother cried
when she saw me. She bathed me, had my hair cut by one of
my numerous uncles, and gave me new clothing she'd made
for me. My boyhood from then on was like that of any other

Zuni boy: school, chopping wood, hauling water, and sheep camp in the summer. I became a crack shot with a .22 rifle around the sheep camp, shooting birds for their feathers. This wasn't sport or juvenile delinquency. The Zuni use feathers to pray as part of every ritual ceremony. The skill saved my life during hand-to-hand combat in the war in Germany. I never shoot a gun now.

My boyhood came to an end in Zuni reckoning when I joined a kiva group. All boys join kiva groups at about the time they enter puberty. There are six of these groups in Zuni; a kiva group is a men's club. In the old days, the men would sit around in the kiva after supper and weave and talk, away from the noise of their wives' houses. Houses were owned by women, and men had no real claim to them. A kiva group's house was a hangout where no women were allowed.

By Zuni tradition, a boy of twelve joins the kiva of the husband of his mother's mid-wife in a coming of age ceremony. He is led into the kiva by a sponsor, a relative who will stand beside him and hold him when the Koko lash him with a yucca whip. Whipping is a ritual act of cleansing and is never used for punishment in Zuni. It sure hurts, though, I remember. When the Koko leave after the initiation, men of the village crowd into the kiva to congratulate the newly-made men and to ask them for a whipping, in turn. That's considered lucky. A boy who has just undergone the kiva initiation ritual is about as pure as anyone can get. The naughtiness characteristic of childhood is not evil; children don't know better when they do something wrong. A newly-made man hasn't had time to get into any trouble yet. An initiate starts out with a clean slate. It may sound strange that old men will ask boys to whip them in blessing, but that's the way we do it in Zuni.

CHAPTER 3

*I*n 1936, when I was in the sixth grade, I heard about the Indian School in Albuquerque, one of the BIA boarding schools, and I thought about having a different lifestyle and learning new things in a big city. My principal, Mrs. Gonzales, sent in an application for me, and my parents agreed to let me go, accepting my desire to broaden my life. These were the good reasons. They were true enough, but there were other, more compelling ones: girls had begun paying attention to me.

In Zuni, boys and girls grow up separately, boys running together and girls staying with their mothers as children. I'd come to think that girls might be interesting long before they had paid any attention to me, but it took me some time to overcome my early years when I'd been undersized. Recently, however, I'd noticed the girls looking at me and looking away, giggling when I caught them at it. There are no secrets at Zuni; soon everyone would notice and the teasing would begin. I had lots of aunts and uncles who would be most unhelpful in any attempt I made to make room in my life for girls. I knew no one in Albuquerque. It would make the whole process much easier.

But when I first went to Albuquerque in the summer of 1937, there were too many other new things to get used to. The city itself was a revelation. I've seen the Empire State

Building in New York, but it didn't make anywhere near the impression on me that seeing the First National Bank Building in Albuquerque did. It was ten stories tall! And I rode a train for the first time, from Gallup to Albuquerque. Even the bus ride from the station to the school was a new experience.

I was placed in a barracks with fifty other boys, keeping my extra clothes in a locker in the basement. That first night I hardly slept at all, wondering if I hadn't made a mistake, leaving my home where everything was familiar.

The next day they tested us and I was placed in the advanced class for seventh grade, mostly because my English was better than most of the other students. We also were assigned vocational training, on the assumption that, as Indians, we probably wouldn't be going to college and we should get something practical out of our school experience. I chose to work at the swine farm, where they fed twenty to thirty hogs to provide meat for the school. One of my uncles kept hogs and I liked them. They smelled bad sometimes, but we kept them clean, and anyway, Indian kids were used to living in a rural setting around animal excrement all the time. At that time, we Indians still had outhouses instead of inside toilets. Smells were just smells. They couldn't hurt you.

Everyone was homesick. For me, it was the food I missed most. I used to write home and ask for Indian bread and roasted corn. I would eat it before I went to bed. It helped me to get to sleep. I had only two dollars with me when I came to Albuquerque, and I spent it all on pop and cinnamon rolls. Nothing else tasted good to me. I remember I was hungry all the time. The school stored corn for the pigs, and I used to secretly roast it and eat it by myself. By the

time I was in the eighth grade, I'd shared my secret with the
three other Zuni boys at the school, for they felt the same
way I did about the school food. But someone told on them,
and they got caught with the roasted corn. I was implicated,
too, even though I wasn't with them that time, and all of us
were punished. We were required to chip the mortar off of
old bricks in our spare time. I don't know what they were
planning to do with the bricks, but each of us had to clean a
thousand of them. We figured we'd cleaned enough bricks
to build a house twenty by fifty, bigger than any house in
Zuni back then. This calculation was the only use I found at
the time for the mathematics I was learning. It gave me little
satisfaction.

My real father, Otto, came to the school to bring me
back to Zuni for Shalako over the Christmas vacation, and
he found me on the brick pile. He thought it was wrong
of the school to punish me for stealing food when I was
hungry. Being hungry was an ever-present threat to Indian
families then. And refusing to give food to someone who
asks for it was one of the reasons that people were hurt by
witches; anger at such a refusal could bring about witch
thoughts in anyone.

By the time I finished the eighth grade, I'd found out
what I wanted to know about girls. They turned out to be
even more interesting than I'd fantasized. The Zuni aren't
puritanical about sex. Mostly, they think of it as another occasion for teasing, and causing laughter, a good thing. And
perhaps I gave it a bigger place in my life when I was young
than I should have, but in retrospect, I don't think so. When
I was hanging around girls, some of my friends were hanging around bars. My addiction, if that's what it was, was
surely healthier in the long run. I became sure of it after I

married Laura. Like the rest of the men my age, I started drinking. She told me she'd lost her first husband to alcoholism and she wasn't about to have it happen again. I stopped. Of course, I'd already stopped chasing women, too, so then I started thinking about politics.

I haven't forgotten my wild days, but to avoid embarrassment to my family, some of whom would be shocked to know how an old man's mind runs, I'm not going to talk about women. Furthermore, since I didn't marry Laura until I was in my thirties, there may be stories even she hasn't heard about my romantic adventures. People like to tell her what they know about me, for she has the best laugh in Zuni. I think what she likes best is laughing at me. I don't need to make it any easier for her.

Even when I was attending the Albuquerque Indian School I came home to Zuni summers and worked with the sheep and cut and hauled wood. I was big enough to do a man's work. Cutting wood took all day. We had to take a team and wagon to where we could find both piñon pine and cedar juniper. The piñon burns too fast if you use it by itself, but in the wintertime you can smell piñon smoke long before you see Zuni. It is still one of the things I like best about living here. Of course, sometimes the smell of piñon meant the women were baking bread or roasting corn, my favorite Indian food. They'd throw the ears of corn, still in their husks and fresh from the fields, right on top of the live coals in the hornos, then seal up the entrances with mud. Next morning, the corn would be ready to eat. I still grow corn every year.

By the time I was in the tenth grade, I could help plow. Farming was a vast change from sheep herding, a lot more work, heavy work, when you don't have a tractor. It would

take two days to plow an acre—and—a—half with a team of
horses. My foster father drove the horses and I held the
plow handles. It was not only difficult, it was boring. Plow-
ing and planting season lasted a month, but then we had
corn, melons, pumpkins in the ground. My foster mother
did her garden with her sisters. The distinction between
men's and women's work is very clearly defined, with the
exception of hauling water. Anyone can haul water. Water is
a holy thing, and it is a blessing to work with it.

I was in Four-H that year. Four-H is an activity something like Boy Scouts, but for farm kids. It was tied into
the high school. As an experiment, I was given two gunny
sacks full of potato seeds, and I harvested a fine crop that
fall. I think I was the first person to grow potatoes in
Zuni. I planted other crops, too, and won prizes with them.
The work interfered with any plans I had for loafing that
summer.

We only had one team of horses and my uncle needed
them, so I used to run the three miles out to the field where
they were kept to bring them back for him. From then on, I
competed in track during the school year at any distance of a
quarter-mile or over. I also played on the baseball team, and
played basketball and touch football.

I ran back and forth from Zuni to the sheep camp in the
summertime, ten miles one way. I even competed in a stick
race once, a race where you kick a stick for twenty-five
miles. It had a religious significance, but people bet on the
outcome, too. I barely found time for girls. I sometimes
hear young people say there's nothing to do, and I don't understand it. There was never enough time to do everything I
wanted to do when I was young.

When I wasn't in school or playing sports or with girls, I

worked. I wanted some nice clothes to impress the girls, so I asked the agent at Black Rock for summer work when I reached seventeen. They put me to work tearing down buildings that the Bureau of Indian Affairs wanted to replace. I ran back and forth from Zuni, about an hour each way, for a dollar—and—a—half a day. I'd give half of it to my mother and spend the rest on candy and clothes, mostly clothes. When I went back to school for my junior year, I thought I was about the grandest thing that walked. Everyone told me how good I looked and how proud they were of me. I agreed with them. I've never had such a high opinion of myself since.

The next summer, I went back to work building fences for the BIA. We cut trees, trimmed them down to fence posts, dug post holes, and strung wire. I made two dollars and sixty cents a day that summer. When I got back to school for senior year, I joined the Federal National Youth Administration program and made six dollars and fifty cents a month, which gave me spending money. I felt rich.

What did a big shot like me do after I graduated? Only four of us made it, two girls and two boys, though we'd started junior year with twelve students. Our folks all were on us all the time to get an education, but not many of us stuck to it. I found out why.

My father said, "You have to go herd sheep again," and hauled me out to sheep camp with my high school diploma in my hand. I guessed my profession was going to be herding sheep. I'd been doing it since I was a kid. The diploma didn't make it any easier.

After a month at sheep camp, I heard that the Bureau was hiring again. A man I'd worked with the previous summer told me. I applied, was hired, and went back to fence build-

ing for the BIA. We stayed out on the job all week long,
from Sunday night to Friday evening, sleeping in sleeping
bags next to the unfinished fence. I was up to three dollars
and ten cents a day, a fortune, particularly since I had little
free time in which to spend it. It was a pity the job didn't last
longer, but it saw me through the rest of the summer.

That fall, there was a good crop of piñon nuts. They
come only once every five or six years, when the conditions
are right for the seeds to mature and germinate. Around the
first week in October, I went out with my mother and father in the wagon to the south side of Zuni Mountain for
two weeks. We sold some of the nuts to the trading store
and kept the rest for our own use. When we returned, I
found that I'd been drafted for World War II.

I reported to the draft board in Gallup, and they sent me
by bus to Santa Fe for the medical examination. I told the
people I wanted to go into the Navy, but x-rays showed I
had once suffered three broken ribs. I explained that I'd
once been kicked by a horse I'd been teasing by tickling her
belly. It served me right. Then I told the doctors about my
running career and that I had had no breathing problems as
a result of the injury, but they weren't impressed. I was
rejected.

Nobody wanted me. I stayed home and did errands for
my mother, chopping wood and carrying water. I worked
with my uncles at farm work and with the sheep and had
nothing different to look forward to. The dreams I had of
being a big shot were pretty much dead. We had good crops
that year, both in the fields and from the sheep. My family
sold the surplus from its harvest along with the wool and
lambs from grandfather's herd. We used our share to buy
our first chairs, tables, and kitchen utensils, bringing our

standard of living almost up to the official level of poverty, if there had been one back then. We still didn't have inside plumbing, but my mother was as proud of her new things as if she'd been featured in *Better Homes and Gardens*. Then I got a new letter from the draft board and this time I passed my physical. The U.S. Army wanted me. It wasn't the Navy, but it was better than sitting around Zuni, or so I thought then. I wondered why the Navy wouldn't take me when there wasn't any walking to do, and the Army would take me when I'd have to hike for many miles, carrying heavy packs. It didn't make any sense then. It doesn't now.

Now that I was about to leave Zuni, the Army suddenly seemed not as wonderful as I thought it might be. The last time I'd been away, to the Albuquerque Indian School, I hadn't liked it all that much. There would be nothing but the white man's food to eat again. I'd have to leave my girl behind, and even if I lived to come back, it would be years from then. I was pretty sure she wouldn't wait. She wanted to get married. Zuni women got married, had children, and ran households. That's what they did then. I couldn't see her putting that off for years. I felt pretty sorry for myself. On the other hand, there were lots of girls out there.

CHAPTER 4

I was wrong about the other women out there. Oh, I saw some in Gallup, where I caught a train to El Paso, but none to talk to. It was months before I talked to anything female. I used to have a coach, who thought if you talked to girls you took the edge off your performance. That was about the same time I had a girl, who thought if you trained on the cinder track four hours a day it took the edge off your performance. They were both wrong.

My induction center was Fort Bliss, Texas. It was huge and noisy. Trucks ran up and down the streets revving their motors and sergeants shouted at everybody, so you didn't have a chance to reflect on what was happening. Maybe that was by design. Most of the guys I was with would have turned around and gone home with a bit of thought. It wasn't long before I wished that horse had kicked me in the head rather than in the ribs.

We got beds and blankets that first night and next day were issued clothes, tested, graded, and assigned for train-ing. I was sent on to Fort Roberts in California before I knew I was going to be trained to be a truck driver. I liked that. I'd driven my uncle's truck around the reservation and it was easier than chopping wood or building fence.

Wrong again. It was a month before I even rode in a

truck. We were told we had to be turned into soldiers before we could be trained at anything. Learning to be a soldier evidently meant getting used to being yelled at. I hated it, but I never said anything. That was the hardest part for me. When we went on ten-mile hikes with full packs, it didn't bother me like it did most of the others. I could have run the whole way. Some of the men were afraid of shooting the guns on the firing range, but it was easy for me. In my mind, I pictured blue jays sitting on the target's bull's eye and aimed for the head, just like at home. At the end of our basic training, I earned an expert rating with the Garand M-1 rifle.

After we'd been in camp a month or two, we could get weekend passes to the small town near the base, but nothing much was going on there for soldiers. The treat was to eat real food instead of what the army served us. I'd have steak; what I wanted was hot tamales and chile. When I was home, I'd never eaten a meal without chile.

We finished basic with field maneuvers survival training, which took us away from the barracks for two weeks. To me, it was like sheep camp. Being an Indian, I had an advantage over the others. They didn't know what hardship was. The best thing about maneuvers, though, was getting away from the yelling. I never did get used to that.

They sent a beer truck out to meet us on maneuvers where we came back to our tent camp each evening. Everybody crowded around, Anglos and Hispanics, pushing to be first. I bought a bottle to see what beer was like; I'd never had any. I decided it smelled like cold horse piss and didn't taste much better. I drank about half the bottle and threw the rest away.

At the end of basic we were sent home on furlough, with orders to report to our new training centers at the end of our leaves. On my first day home I asked my mother for hot tamales and chile and ate like I'd been starved for all the time I'd been gone. In truth, I had been—for real food, anyway. I strutted around town in my uniform, visiting relatives, and everybody told me how handsome I looked in it. I hadn't felt so good about myself since I'd been a junior in high school with new clothes.

Before I left, my uncle gave me corn meal to pray with and told me prayers I had to say every day to keep from being hurt. He said if I ran out of corn meal I was to write home and get more. He said I'd be going where there were people dying and maybe I'd have to kill people myself. I'd go crazy unless I kept my heart straight with prayer. That scared me more than the idea of getting killed, myself. I promised I'd do as he said.

I was a day late reporting to my new post, Fort Sill, Oklahoma, and worried all the way that I'd end up in the stockade. That's what they called jail in the army: stockade. We had been threatened with stockade all through basic training and were even marched by one once to see it. It was just a hogwire fence enclosure with guard towers at each end. The guys inside came to the fence as we walked by, some making cat calls and whistling, some begging for cigarettes. I decided being inside would be worse than what we were doing, yelling and all.

They didn't pay any attention to my being late, just sent me over to the field artillery unit I'd been assigned to. I was there for less than half a year, but it seemed like forever. I sweated all day long, and it was so hot at night in the wooden barracks that I couldn't sleep. The training was hard. But I was still stronger than other people from the heavy work I'd done all my life. Some of the men suffered. We fired the big guns, the 155 millimeter howitzers, with training rounds. They made so much noise I wondered what full loads would sound like. I figured I'd be deaf by the time the war was over.

The army wasn't satisfied with me yet, so it sent me to Fort Raleigh in North Carolina for another year of training. I didn't learn anything new. From there, I was sent to Camp Van Dorn in Mississippi to join the 63rd Infantry Division, which was recruiting enough men to bring it up to full strength for assignment overseas. I thought I'd finally found my home in the army.

I was so bored with training, even the prospect of frontline duty looked good. Maybe that was by design, too, but it would be giving the army more foresight than I'd seen anyone with bars on their shoulders exhibit up to then. I never met an officer I had much respect for as a person. We sometimes had lectures about what they called the "big picture" from officers using pointers and maps. The maps were so small that they showed almost no detail. The arrows painted on the maps showing advances and retreats were so wide they covered what would be hundreds of miles on the ground, most of it unpaved. But I knew the army required paved roads for such maneuvers. In some of the country around Zuni, even tanks would get stuck eventually if they left the roads, and that country is drier than any place in Europe. None of the lecturers knew what they were talking about. I hoped the generals in charge were smarter.

We took a train to Camp Shanks, New York, to be shipped to Europe. The day before we left Shanks, my cheek puffed up like something had bitten me and they put me in the hospital. My "home in the army" left without me. A week later, I was put on a bus for New York with some others who had been left behind for one reason or another. In

New York we boarded a U.S. Navy destroyer. I finally had a
look at Navy life.

Below deck, there were hammocks strung from the floor
to the ceiling, and I was assigned a top one I could reach by
climbing a ladder built into a hammock support post. They
let us go back up on deck as we sailed out of New York harbor, and my last glimpse of land was the Statue of Liberty
and the New York skyline. The windows in the tall buildings
glinted in the sunset. None of it looked real.

After breakfast the next morning, I went on deck thinking I would still be able to see the city. All I could see was
water, miles and miles of water. Water is sacred, but this
was too much of it. I wondered why the sea was so full and
we always had to worry about enough rain in Zuni to make
a crop.

Five days out we hit a storm and the destroyer swung
from side to side, its nose going up in the air then diving
into the sea. I had tried riding bulls when I was in high
school, thinking I might become a famous rodeo performer.
It was like that, only it didn't stop after the ten seconds you
were supposed to stay on the bull. It went on and on and on.
We weren't allowed on deck. It was too dangerous. They
said we could go overboard and there would be no chance
of being picked up out of the sea.

I didn't care. I was seasick. It was the sickest I've ever
been in my life, the nausea, the dizziness, worse than any
possible hangover. I couldn't eat, I couldn't sleep, I couldn't
even rest. All I could do was vomit until my stomach was
sore. I never saw any sailors below deck in our section, but
the few soldiers who didn't get sick were kept busy cleaning
up the floors and the toilets. There was vomit everywhere.
Some of the guys were too sick to get out of their ham-

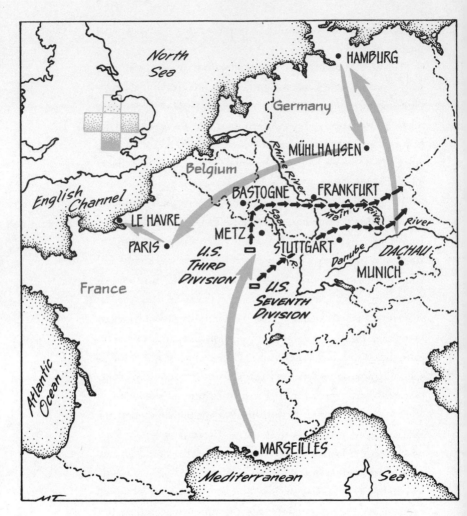

Virgil Wyaco's Travels, European Theater, 1944–1945. Map by Michael Taylor.

mocks. Even today, I know I could never go through that
again.

The storm lasted two days and then it was smooth sailing, if you were a sailor, maybe. I wondered why I ever thought I wanted to join the Navy. I didn't fully recover until after we docked at Marseilles in southern France and went ashore. The trip lasted twelve days. I wondered if I would get lucky and be killed so I wouldn't have to face going back. Maybe, if I lived, I would find some way to stay in Europe.

We were in a camp outside of Marseilles for about a week before they loaded us on planes and flew us to Metz, in France, to a replacement depot. All of us were replacements, being sent to fill the vacancies left by casualties. I didn't know anybody. I'd thought to go into battle with friends on either side, knowing they'd try to take care of me. Being a replacement for someone already dead made the war almost unreal. Well, the Zunis live in the present: the past is gone and the future has not come, but they are all connected. It is only the present you have to concern yourself with, though. It was the present that worried me. I hoped the corn-meal prayers would keep me from being one of those for whom a replacement was needed.

In Metz, I was loaded into a truck with other replacements and sent to the front lines. I thought the others would be able to hear my heart pound, it was beating so loudly. I could smell fear sweat and knew some of it was mine. They issued me new clothing and a .30-caliber carbine. I'd qualified with it, but it had never been my principal weapon. I was assigned to the Fourth Infantry Division, 8th Regiment, Company B. All the training in heavy weapons had been pointless. I was a rifleman. We could hear the shelling night and day, and at first that was the worst of it. Not so bad. If this was all I had to worry about, I could get used to it. I even found I could sleep through the noise. To be on the safe side, I used my corn meal and prayed. My heart slowed down to a normal pace. I was wrong to relax. The unit I'd joined had been building up its strength after suffering heavy losses trying to break through the Siegfried Line and being thrown back. They'd been waiting for me, I guess, for before I could get used to sitting around, Company B was up to full strength and we were put back into the line in time for a new attack on the Siegfried Line. We went in at the same place we'd been thrown out of last time, east of Metz. I could see why it had been so hard; the Germans fought fiercely. We didn't even reach the Siegfried Line before we were pinned down by machine-gun fire. My heart was jumping like it wanted to get out of my body and hide someplace. I'd have gone with it if I could. There was no place to run to; I just lay on the ground for hours and thought about being a mole or gopher . . . something that could dig into the earth. My hope was that it would get dark soon so the Germans couldn't see me and I could get out of there, but our artillery knocked out the machine guns and we were sent forward again.

We captured the Line and crossed the Saar River, marching fast toward Bastogne in Belgium. The Germans had broken through American lines and were threatening to outflank our forces, even rolling us back into the sea. Our unit was transferred from the Seventh Army Command to Third Army Command under General Patton. We were uneasy. We all knew General Patton's reputation. He was successful as a commander, but less careful about his troops than other commanders. For him, winning was everything. Our chances of getting killed just went up. History books call the campaign of the winter of '44 in Belgium the "Battle of the Bulge."

Winter set in with cold and blowing snow. Our advance slowed to less than thirty miles a day. An artillery shell that burst a few feet away damaged my hearing and left me with rumbling sounds in my left ear. We were subsisting on "C" rations: no hot food. By the time we got within thirty miles of Bastogne, over three-quarters of our original unit had been killed and the holes filled with inexperienced replacements. By this time, I was looked on as an experienced soldier by the green troops joining us.

The Germans were focusing a steady barrage of artillery fire on our unit as we advanced. Any leader but Patton would have pulled us back, given our losses, but the 101st Airborne Division was trapped near Bastogne and Patton was determined to go to their relief. The closer we got, the worse it was. A machine gunner who had been giving us some cover from small arms fire was killed right next to me. It got so bad, I took over. No one likes to be a machine gunner because they have to sit in one place, partly exposed and with all the enemy riflemen targeting on them. Some officer must have seen me, because the Army later gave me a Bronze Star. That wasn't why I did it. The Germans were coming right at us and we were in danger of being overrun. I didn't know about the medal until I read it on my discharge papers.

It was nearly Christmas when we finally captured Bastogne, and General Patton came to congratulate us. It was the first time I'd seen him. Generals don't show up until the fighting is over. I'd been under fire for more than thirty days. I'd found it wasn't something you could get used to.

We rested a few days and then the Germans counter-attacked. I killed my first man. He came straight toward me, as if he'd decided I was the one he wanted to kill. I've seen coyotes do that with sheep, running past some to get to a particular lamb. He aimed to fire, but I shot first and he fell. I found that shooting a man is not like shooting a blue jay. I killed my second and third Germans in the next two or three days of fighting. I couldn't sleep the night I killed the first man; I kept seeing him coming at me and then falling down. What if he'd gotten up? I kept thinking about it. By the time I'd killed the third man, I stopped thinking about it. I was still alive, at least.

We had Christmas dinner in Bastogne, a hot meal with turkey and everything else. My outfit celebrated right through New Year's. I don't know where they found all the liquor, but everyone but me got drunk. All I took were a couple of shots of cognac. If the Germans had attacked then, they would have won because we were in no condition to resist. I made a friend during the time we were in Bastogne, a white man named Jackson. It made the fighting easier to bear when you could look up and catch someone's eye and nod. It made the whole experience a little less unreal.

After New Year's, we were told we had to cross the Rhine. Before we ever reached the Rhine, I fell into another river I don't remember the name of and got my feet wet. My feet were cold all day. Cold, wet feet are dangerous; you can get trench foot. That will disable you as fast as a bullet. We came to a town for the night but couldn't build a fire, so we put blankets over the windows of a house and lit candles we found there. I was able to get my wet shoes and socks off and rub my feet warm. I took off the top part of my longjohns and cut the arms off to use as socks, a trick I'd learned in sheep camp when I was a kid. It was too damp and cold to dry the wet socks.

By the second or third week in January, we were close to the Rhine River, near Frankfurt. We were told we would be crossing there and could see wave after wave of bombers flying over every day to blow up the German fortifications along the river. It was March before they got us up and moved us down to the river bank early one morning. There were boats waiting for us and we realized this was the day. Our names were called in alphabetical order to board. For some reason, they started with the W's and I was the first one called. Fighter planes blanketed the other shore with smoke in the hope that the Germans wouldn't see us. How dumb could the Germans be? We'd never smoked the river before. Our intentions couldn't have been clearer if we'd sent them a letter. I hoped the corn meal had created a little pocket of Zuni all around me that the bullets couldn't get through.

I felt exposed out there, like a crow in a snowdrift. I was in the first wave and waited for the artillery and machine-gun fire I was sure would break our boats up. I'm not much of a swimmer, particularly carrying a rifle and full field pack. We reached the opposite bank and started moving up, followed by the second wave of boats. The third wave took heavy fire and we could hear the men screaming as they were hurt or their boats were blown up. There was nothing we could do about it. If they'd started with the A's instead of the W's, I'd never have made it across.

We started marching inland towards Frankfurt, over more or less flat terrain, not mountainous country like what I'd seen of France. The tanks and trucks crossed the river after we did, and followed us until they passed us to lead the at-tack. They circled the city and blasted it, leaving it to us to clean up. All we saw were dead Germans, some with their heads blown off. There was fresh blood stinking every-where. It was the same town after town; it made me sick. We destroyed Stuttgart, another big city, just as we had de-stroyed Frankfurt.

Toward the end of April, our colonel told us the Germans were defeated and were getting ready to surrender, but we kept on fighting, moving thirty or forty miles a day. Every time we thought we could rest, the colonel would say, "One more town." That's what we called him, "Colonel One More Town."

I'd never realized there were so many people in Germany: every five or ten miles there was a town of five or ten thousand people. Germany was not much bigger than New Mexico but had sixty times as many people. Everything was arranged to make the most use of the least space so they could all fit it. Even the trees I saw were planted in straight rows.

The first week in April, we were outside Munich and were transferred back to the Seventh Army. General Patton wanted his Third Army to go north toward Berlin. We captured Munich in the last heavy fighting our unit saw, and I killed my last German in combat, the seventh I was sure of. I can't remember where I got four through six anymore. I'd fired at others, but I didn't know whether I'd killed them or not; I didn't see them fall. That was rifle fire. Machine-gun fire is different. You don't know what damage you're doing to the enemy when you shoot a machine gun. It's almost impersonal. You don't aim. I didn't keep track of the casualties I'd inflicted with the machine gun, but I know I hurt some people then.

My friend Jackson was wounded in the fighting around Munich and sent back to the M.A.S.H. hospital. I don't know whether he lived or not. I never saw him again.

As soon as we'd secured Munich, we liberated Dachau, the concentration camp a few miles away. It was my worst experience of war, of my life, really. I'd seen men next to me killed almost every day. The towns and cities we

smashed through were filled with dead people. But I'd
seen nothing like Dachau. There were dead people piled everywhere, sometimes in neat rows the way Germans like
things, sometimes all twisted, when they froze before they
could be straightened out. Those looked like juniper fire-
wood just unloaded from a pickup truck, no more human
than that, all naked and skinny. Those that were still alive
looked like they ought to be dead. I'd never seen people
more grateful for food.

And I'd never been more angry in my life. Nor have I
been since. To the Zuni, death is a transition time that must
be handled with love and respect by one's closest family. A
person's body and hair must be washed, rubbed with corn
meal, and pointed to the west toward Kothluwalawa, with
prayers to guide the departed spirit on the way. The Navajo
fear death and believe the spirits of the dead want to harm
the living. We know better.

Where were the families of all these dead people? What
kind of people were these Germans to let bodies be treated
this way? The Zuni don't even kill birds without asking permission. Who asked permission of these dead people to take
their lives?

The camp had been guarded by SS troops. They surrendered without firing a shot, about sixty of them. They were
standing and sitting around, under guard, about fifty yards
outside the camp when old Colonel One More Town came
up, pointing and saying, "You, you and you!" to a dozen of
us. I was one he pointed to; I followed him. He led us up to
the SS troops and ordered "Shoot them!," pointing this time
at the SS troops. I didn't wait for another order, nor did any
of the other men. The dozen of us all emptied our clips,
shooting into the Germans. It took less than half a minute before they were like the same jumbled pile of bodies we'd

found inside. The colonel turned and walked away, and so did the rest of us, leaving the men guarding them in shock.

The colonel ordered that the bodies be left there to rot, and no one argued with him. I've never felt any remorse for my part in that execution. Those SS guards were more like witches than like men. They'd already lived too long.

Winter was over and we stopped wearing overcoats, so I could run faster when I had to. Carrying ammunition and a pack over an overcoat makes a person slow and easy to shoot. We went back to Munich from Dachau, much shaken. Our squad took shelter in what would have been a family-owned general store back home. There were canned goods on the shelves and a wood stove, which we fired up. Then we fixed ourselves a feast, spreading it out on the counter from the stores we found in the shop. Just when we were ready to sit down to eat, a German artillery shell came right through the window and exploded, blowing our feast away. It seemed fitting, somehow.

We were tired. Our unit had been fighting continually since November, six months back, without relief. We were so tired, some of our men were making mistakes, standing when they should have been hugging the earth. Some of them had been killed for not being alert. The critical phase of the war was over, so our army command sent us thirty miles south, away from the fighting, to recover. If things went bad, we could be moved from reserve status and sent back into the thick of it. Just to be out of the sound of gunfire was restful to us, however.

Two weeks later we were sent to Hamburg and then on to Muhlheiser, but our placement there was strategic only. There was no more fighting. Berlin had fallen. On May 7, 1945, the Germans surrendered. The war in Europe was over.

CHAPTER 5

*T*he formal signing of the surrender took place on May 8, 1945, and suddenly we had nothing to do but wait for the Army to decide where we would go next. We were told that the war in the Pacific against Japan was going well, but it would take months, even years, to wind up, for the Japanese would never surrender until we invaded their home islands. As seasoned troops, we could expect to be part of the last big push, but first we would be sent back to the States to be retrained and re-outfitted. Assignment to the Pacific theater would follow. It sounded like more boredom, to be followed by more crunching fear.

All we could think about then was going home. Whatever came after would come. Our mail caught up with us, but it didn't make anything easier for most of the guys. Those who got good news could hardly wait to get back, and those who got bad news wondered why they had fought so hard. I had good news. My brother, Lee, had joined the Navy and was in the Pacific, but was still all right. It took me two days to read everything. I got lots of letters and clothes and stuff like that, warm socks and sweaters. I could have used them earlier. I even got birthday presents; I'd turned twenty-one on February 17. Where had I been? Frankfurt? Stuttgart? I told some of the guys and they teased me about finally becoming a man. What else had I been when I shot those first three Germans outside Bastogne? Most of these guys were replacements, who hadn't even joined us until later.

My mother and sisters and aunts had sent me cookies, all crushed, but I guess they'd been thinking about me. I also got another packet of corn meal. I'd been running low, using just little pinches to offer the gods. The corn meal had worked. I'd gone through some of the fiercest fighting of the war and never had a scratch, or even a cold. It was my own secret weapon.

I also had some bad news. The girl I'd left back home had found another guy, like I thought she might. Part of it was my fault. I'd promised to write every day, but that hadn't been possible over the past months in Europe. There were letters and even Christmas presents from her in the pile of mail, and then suddenly nothing until the "Dear John" letter was written. I wrote back to all the people who'd written me, telling them I'd been busy and had just received everything, but I didn't write to her.

The Army didn't seem to believe the war was over. Maybe they thought the Germans would rearm and come at us again. I even heard we were going to fight the Russians next instead of the Japanese. Most of the men talking that way were fairly new to the outfit. The rest of us had learned not to pay any attention to that kind of talk. The command generals never told anyone what they were going to do next, so if you heard about it in advance it was probably untrue.

Finally, in July, they told us we were going back to the States and loaded us into boxcars. It took us three days to go from Muhlheiser, in Germany, to Paris, France. We should have used boxcars to advance against the Germans; it would have taken less time. When we got to Paris, old Colonel One More Town came to see us and warn us there was a lot of venereal disease in Paris. He said we shouldn't take any chances about bringing it home with us. Then we were issued pro kits, venereal disease prevention kits, with condoms and tubes of salve that you were supposed to use after having sex. I never even tried to figure out how they worked. I never needed it. The idea of paying somebody to have sex was ridiculous. Hey, I was the great Zuni lover, right? I thought I'd just wait until I got home. In Paris, you could have a three-day pass to town by just asking for it, but I didn't go. I stayed in camp and waited. Anyway, maybe the colonel was right.

We weren't in Paris long, the way the army figures time, only about two weeks. Then we were loaded into trucks and transferred to Le Havre to catch a ship back to the States. We actually boarded in the last week of July. I can't say I was eager to be at sea again, remembering what happened last time, but I kept the thought of going back to Zuni in my mind. This was a bigger ship, the USS Heritage. It didn't wallow much, even when we hit bad weather. Maybe that's why I didn't get sick again.

We knew we were home when we saw the Statue of Liberty in New York Harbor waiting for us. Everyone was shouting and waving, much different than when we'd left. We'd been pretty quiet then. They had us off the ship, into trucks, and back in Camp Shanks by noon. I'd never seen the army move so fast. The camp commanders greeted us and told us to throw our old "C" rations away, because we'd be eating steak for supper, and they kept their promise. That was a first, too.

Within a week, they'd processed us all, sending us to the army posts nearest our homes. I was on a train for three days before I got back to Fort Bliss, Texas, the first week in August. Almost the first thing they did was to give us our back pay. I'd drawn partial pay of ten dollars only twice in all the time I'd been gone, and that's all the money I'd seen. I hadn't needed it. I was surprised when they figured up how much they owed me. First, base pay for a private was fifty dollars a month. I'd been promoted twice: to private first class and corporal, and each promotion came with a pay raise. I'd been given the Infantry Combat Badge, which was worth another ten dollars a month. Overseas pay and combat pay both added bonus money. I had hundreds of dollars in my hand when I left the pay tent. They said there'd be more when I came back from furlough. To celebrate, I got a pass to El Paso, the town nearest the post, and found a good Mexican cafe where I could get a bowl of chile and some enchiladas. I made a hog of myself, but it was sure good.

It took three or four days to process the paperwork for my thirty-day furlough to Zuni. That was the army I was used to. Before I left the post, the papers were filled with news about the dropping of the atomic bomb on Hiroshima. They were predicting the end of the war. That was all right with me, but I didn't believe it.

I called Zuni and left word for my uncle and my sisters that I'd be taking the bus to Gallup and when it would arrive, as there was no public transportation from Gallup to Zuni. When I arrived in Gallup, my uncle was waiting for me in his pickup truck. He had a medicine man with him, a man I knew. Before we crossed the Zuni River, my uncle stopped the truck and the medicine man blessed me with corn meal, brushing me down with an eagle wing fan, taking

away all the evil I might have brought with me from where
I'd been. They didn't want me to bring disease back to the
pueblo. They wrapped up whatever they found in corn husk
and had me throw it into the river. I think maybe the medicine men can see whatever it is they clean you of, but I
don't know.

My mother cried when I came into the house, she was so
glad I was home. She'd fixed everything I liked to eat.
People came to see me, and I visited everyone wearing my
uniform with my corporal stripes. It was just like on my last
furlough, except this time everyone wanted to know about
the fighting. I didn't want to talk about it, so I just gave general answers, which worked just as well. Even my old girl-
friend, the one who sent me the "Dear John" letter, talked
to me and asked me to come back to her. I said no. Even
though we heard the war was over with Japan, I knew I'd
have to go back in the army, and I didn't want a wife cheat-
ing on me at home.

Anyway, I found a new girl. I went to the Gallup Ceremonial, a fiesta held once a year where Indian people from
all over the country go for four days and have dances and
stick races and horse races. It was just for Indians back then,
though white people used to pay to sit in the grandstand and
watch. I met a Navajo girl I liked and stayed with her all during the Ceremonial. She promised to write to me.

A week after the Ceremonial I had to go back to Fort
Bliss. Everyone in Zuni thought I'd be home again in a few
days, but I knew better. I was three days' late getting back,
but they just yelled at me. I knew they wouldn't do anything
to me. They shipped me to Camp Bulkner in North Carolina for jungle training. The army thought we'd still have to
defeat the Japanese on each of the Pacific Islands they held.

They didn't trust the Japanese at all. I don't think the army was ready to have the war end so fast. They'd made all these plans to deploy the troops from Europe to the Pacific, and didn't want to admit it wasn't necessary.

Our colonel didn't work us very hard because he knew it was all a waste of time. I used to go on leave to Greensboro every weekend and eat steak. I got paid every month now. We sat around until February before I received orders to go back to Fort Bliss for discharge. There I sat around some more, doing very little, until April, when I actually was separated from the army.

I asked my uncle to pick me up at Gallup again and went back to being an Indian. I hauled wood, herded sheep, and helped with the crops. I even helped take care of my uncle's hogs, as I'd learned at the Albuquerque Indian School. We cut and baled alfalfa for the horses, heavy dirty work. Little bits of hay got under my shirt and itched, just like the old days.

The Navajo woman that I'd met at the Gallup Ceremonial wrote to me as she'd promised, and I brought her over to Zuni. The women in my family didn't like it much. The only friends the Navajo have among the Pueblo Indians are the Jemez and that goes all the way back to the Pueblo Revolt in the seventeenth century. Because the Navajo gave them help back in 1680, the Jemez were the only Pueblo Indians that didn't join Kit Carson when he rounded up the Navajo and imprisoned them at the Bosque Redondo in 1864.

To the Zuni, the Navajo are "the enemy." A hundred years ago, when we had an active scalp society, the scalps were understood to be Navajo scalps. I told the women in my family that, in the old days, when a warrior brought

back an enemy woman for his wife, she was accepted by his
family. It might even have been true once. Anyway, we had
a son and she named him after me, Virgil Wyaco, Jr.

I was just drifting and I wanted to do something with my
life, so I decided to go to the University of New Mexico on
the G.I. Bill and study to become an electrical engineer. I
had visions of bringing electricity to Zuni. The G.I. Bill only
paid ninety dollars a month, so I didn't have enough money
to bring my wife with me. I left her in Zuni, where she and
the baby would be looked after. It didn't work out. There
were too many differences culturally for her and my family
to get along. She got homesick and went back to St. Mi-
chaels, Arizona, where she was born. I knew her family and
felt she and my son would be all right with them. The
Navajo are like the Zuni in some ways. The women own almost everything. The worst part was that I almost lost track
of my son. My wife didn't have to file papers or anything,
because we'd been married Indian fashion. She could just
walk out when she wanted to.

In Albuquerque, I first lived at the Indian school, but
when the new students came they said I'd have to leave. I
found a place to sleep in the basement of a private house,
along with other ex-G.I.'s who were also on the G.I. Bill.
I made friends like Cal Riley and Jay Jones, who I still see.
A lot of anthropologists at the University were good to me
because I was an Indian. I used to babysit for Dr. John
Adair's children and always looked forward to going there
because he fed me. Sometimes, I took Jones with me. Neither one of us was eating too good on the G.I. Bill.

I also worked for Dr. Florence Hawley, the anthropologist, helping with anything she could find for me to do to
make a little spending money. I was pretty active socially at

the time, and that was expensive. I borrowed money some-times from Jones, telling him I'd pay him when my grand-father sold the wool. By this time, we were roommates, living in Albuquerque's Martineztown barrio. I didn't tell him they wouldn't sell the wool until spring, so I had quite a debt to pay when my money finally came. I think he was be-ginning to wonder if he'd ever get paid back, but he didn't say anything.

I took college math and bookkeeping and English. The only one that was hard was English, and I had Jones write my English theme papers. He just gave them to me. One, I entered into a radio contest on "my most embarrassing mo-ment." Jones wrote about something that had happened to him in the army. He got diarrhea from eating cherries and washing dishes with yellow soap at the same time. When he went on sick call, he didn't want to shout out what was wrong, so he whispered. The admitting clerk thought he said he had gonorrhea rather than diarrhea. They almost locked him up before he straightened it out. That won me twenty-five dollars' worth of groceries. Another of Jones's stories, about Joe Crazyhorse, was submitted by my English teacher to the *Thunderbird*, the University literary magazine. They published it, under my name of course. I don't know if Jones thought it was as funny as I did.

I learned more outside of class than in class, though the bookkeeping course came in handy later. Engineering stu-dents told me I was in the wrong field if I wanted to be an electrician. Engineers work in factories, not out in rural areas designing electrical systems for housing. They told me what I really wanted was to become an electrical contrac-tor. They said there was only one way to become one: work for some years as a state-licensed electrician's helper and

then take a licensing test. In order to qualify to take the
test, you had to have the licensed electrician sign an affi-
davit swearing you'd put in your time. They also said that
the trade skills—carpentry, masonry, and others, as well
as electrical contracting—were controlled by Whites and
Mexicans. A licensed, skilled craftsman was most likely to
take his own son, or nephew, as a helper. That's still true.
back then, there weren't any Zuni electrical contractors
I could apprentice to, and neither the Mexicans nor the
Whites wanted to let Indians into the trade.

At that time, even though I'd risked my life fighting
overseas, I could neither vote nor drink alcohol in New
Mexico under state law because I was an Indian. When we'd
go once a week for supper at the Pig Stand Cafe, across
from the University, I'd ask for a beer and a soup and sand-
wich to tease the waitress and make the others laugh. I
didn't really want the beer because I still didn't like the taste
of it. But if the State of New Mexico wouldn't even let me
buy a beer, I figured I didn't have much chance of making
them give me an opportunity to become an electrician.

I dropped out of school and got a job in a factory in Albuquerque, making venetian blinds. After a few months there,
I applied to Maisel's Indian Trading Post and got a job
making silver and turquoise jewelry. At Maisel's, I became
friends with a Santa Domingo Indian. He'd heard about a
job in Los Alamos, planting shrubs and flowers for Baker
Brothers Nursery, that paid better. It was outside work, so
we went to work there. That ended when winter came. I
went back to Zuni, no farther along in my search for a career than when I started.

The following spring the superintendent of the Bureau of
Indian Affairs told me about a job as maintenance man for

the Civil Aeronautics Administration office in Black Rock. I applied and got the job, working there for three years to save up enough money to buy a three-quarter ton pickup truck. We needed the truck to haul wood and farm supplies. On the job, I learned something about the maintenance of motors and generators, which was interesting to me because they ran with electricity. I felt I was getting closer to what I wanted to do.

My other responsibility at the CAA was to climb to the top of Dowa Yallane, where there was a beacon, and change the light bulb on the tower when it burned out. It took me almost a day to climb the mountain and come back. My boss used to say: "Take the rest of the day off. It was more than a day's work." He was a good boss.

Things were looking up. The tribe appointed me book-keeper, which was easy for me because I'd taken bookkeep-ing at UNM. There wasn't much in the way of revenue back then. From time to time, I'd give a financial report at a council meeting. It was my first taste of politics and I liked it. The veterans organized a local American Legion Post and I was elected vice-commander. Pretty good for a corporal. The girls still thought I was good-looking, so even that was all right.

I got laid off in May of 1951 and started looking for a job again. In the meantime, there was still plenty of work in the field helping my father haul alfalfa, watermelons, and canta-loupes to Gallup to sell. The melons went for fifteen to twenty cents apiece. It was good money then. The rest we gave away to relatives, so they wouldn't go to waste.

The waiting started bothering me. I didn't want to just work for my father the rest of my life. By 1953, I was sick. I had developed stomach trouble and was nervous and short-

tempered. I had nightmares about combat. My mother and
father were worried about me. They said my condition
came from seeing all those dead bodies and being shot at.
John Adair, the anthropologist I used to babysit for when I
went to school at UNM, was working in Zuni and he noticed it, too. A friend of his from Cornell University came
visiting him, and he said if it were not taken care of I could
go crazy and eventually die of it. They call it post-combat
syndrome now.

My parents asked my grandfather to help me. He belonged to the Newekwe clown society, and they knew how
to cure problems like mine. He started me on a four-day
cure that began each morning when he'd come to the house
and mix herbs for me to drink. I'd vomit four times before
noon. At the end of the fourth day, he told me I'd get over
it. He was right. My parents noticed that over the next
two months I showed signs of improving. I no longer had
nightmares and had started treating them with respect, not
showing temper like I had before.

When you get cured by the Newekwe, you have to join
the society. There are two levels, the clowns who attend the
masked dances, with whom everyone is familiar, and the
officers, who know how to cure. I became a clown. The
clowns represent the people, just as the masked dancers
represent the gods. Since the first times, the people keep
forgetting the instructions the gods gave them about how to
live and the clowns act out the mistakes, getting everything
backward. Sometimes, they also make fun of people who
cause scandal in the pueblo. They talk pretty dirty, but the
people laugh. I performed whenever I was asked.

I was thirty years old in 1954 and had about given up any
thought of doing anything in the world. It looked like I'd be

a traditional Zuni Indian, like my father and grandfather. There was nothing wrong with that. It just wasn't what I'd planned for my life.

The Bureau of Indian Affairs brought electricity to the pueblo and I didn't have anything to do with it. I didn't like what happened because of it. When masked dances were held, the young people would stay inside the houses listening to rock and roll music on their radios instead of watching. I don't like rock music even now.

Before the war, young boys depended on their older brothers and uncles for guidance. The younger ones were patient, waiting until they came of age to take their places in the society. But for three years during the war most of the young men had been taken from the pueblo in the draft. While they were away, there was no one for the young boys to look up to and follow. And when the veterans came back, most of them had drinking problems, so they weren't good role models anyway. The young people didn't ask them for help because they couldn't even help themselves. When electricity came in, it brought radio and the young people all wanted to follow white role models. The new music became the symbolic defining difference between the young and the old. The generation gap is still there.

I kept looking for work away from the pueblo, dissatisfied with what was happening to Zuni and to me. Finally, I heard there were job openings at the Fort Wingate Army Depot, just east of Gallup. After a job interview and some waiting, I got a letter to report for work on August 11, 1954. I was on my way.

From left to right: Alice Tekala (Virgil's aunt), Virgil Wyaco, and his mother,
Esther Tekala, 1947.

Virgil Wyaco, 1946. Return from overseas, Germany, World War II. (above)

Virgil Wyaco. Photo taken Feb. 1943, Basic Training, Camp Roberts, California. (upper right)

Wyaco medals. From left to right: Bronze Star Medal, Combat Infantry Medal, Good Conduct Medal, World War II Victory Medal, World War II European Theater Operation Medal, Occupational World War II Germany, and World War II Overall European Germany-France Operational Medal. (lower right)

Tribal Council, 31 December 1970. From left to right: Mecalita Wychucy [?], Bernand Bowekaty, Governor Robert Lewis, Lt. Governor Theodore Edaakia, Harold Tucson, Virgil Wyaco, Chester Gasper, Dennis Nash. (above)

Virgil and Laura Wyaco, 1972. (upper right)

Virgil Wyaco, newly appointed postmaster, 1971. (lower right)-

Esther Tekala, Virgil's Mother. Photo taken 1978.

*SIPI Graduation, 1986. An unknown Zuni girl accepts
her diploma from Superintendent Chores Robert. Virgil Wyaco,
Chairman of the Board of SIPI Regents, stands
to the right. (upper)*

*Speaking at Phoenix, Arizona, 1986, PHS. Campaign for
Non-smoking. Zuni received award. (lower)*

Virgil with Dowa Yalanne in background, summer 1995.
Photo by Victoria R. Evans. (above)

Virgil at home, Zuni, Summer 1995.
Photo by Victoria R. Evans. (upper right)

From left to right: Candy A. Wyaco, Donald K. Wyaco,
Katheryn R. Nidiffer, and grandson Jonathan I. Nidiffer.
(lower right)

Candy Wyaco and fiancé, Clif Cypert, 1996

Virgil's daughter Pamela and her husband Steve Moore. Grandsons Chad and Chase. Atlanta, Georgia, 1995.

CHAPTER 6

W hen I left Zuni I had my pickup truck, my silversmithing tools, and my clothes. I didn't know if I was ever coming back. This sense of alienation had been growing for a long time, not just since my return from the war. I'd made choices early in my life without knowing what the consequences would be later on, and no one ever warned me. My family was proud of me for venturing away from Zuni when I went to Albuquerque for my seventh and eighth grades of school. They were proud of me when I won races in high school, and when I was one of the few who stuck with school long enough to graduate. They were proud of me when I went into the service, and when I came back a hero. They were proud of me when I helped organize the American Legion post in Zuni and became one of the top officers. They were proud of me when I served as the tribe's fiscal officer for three years. None of this was of any use to me as a Zuni.

All of the time I was excelling at this or that, other men of my age were making different choices. They chose to drop out of school and live as traditional Zunis. They chose to stay out of the army and accept draft deferments as priests in training. They chose to serve the gods.

By the time I was thirty, they were thirty. They were

Zuni, becoming important in the religious life of the pueblo. I didn't know what I was.

I have known a number of anthropologists well: John Adair, Jack Roberts, Florence Hawley, Ed Dozier, Carroll Riley, and Jay Jones. I've read what the early anthropologists had to say about Zuni: Cushing, Stephenson, Parsons, Kroeber, and Bunzel. I know what anthropologists know about the Zuni. Where I have personal knowledge, the facts are mostly right, but the essence is mostly wrong. To understand, you have to speak the language, because so much is contained in the way Zuni think. They express their perceptions of reality differently than English-speakers do. The line-for-line translations of Zuni chants that Bunzel published read like nonsense in English. In Zuni, they are poetic in their beauty, clarity, and simplicity. It was this life of the spirit that I was closed off from.

The boldness I exhibited as a child, the approval I sought as a youth for my athletic and school activities, the distinction with which I served in the war all marked me as someone not fit by temperament to be a priest. When I was inducted into the clown society, it sealed me away from the sacred world. Most observers of Zuni ceremonies believe the clowns make fun of others to provide sanctions against inappropriate behavior. They are more than that. They mock the gods themselves. Even most Zuni have no idea how frightening that is. Who knows what the gods make of this? What happens when a clown dies? Is his spirit accepted in Kothluwalawa?

There are always ten clowns at any performance in which the gods appear, and the leadership of the clown society selects which individuals will portray one or another of them, for they are all different, with different personalities.

The clown personalities present stereotypes of incorrect be- / 53
havior: cowardice, stupidity, anger, filthy talk, and the like.
I am surprised that some anthropologist hasn't written that
they are merely Passion Play figures engrafted on some
ancient aboriginal ritual form, like the depiction of the
Chapeyeka among the Yaqui of Sonora during Easter week.
Maybe someone has.

For the Zuni, the clowns represent the people as they
were before the gods instructed them in correct behavior.
The behavior they exhibit is disgusting. Stephenson wrote,
at the turn of the century, that she had seen the clowns eat
feces and drink urine during ritual performances. She wrote
that they bit the heads off living mice and ate them. She said
that they killed dogs and dismembered them with their
hands and teeth, eating the raw intestines, like wolves.
Well, maybe. But who would do such things if the gods did
not require it to help the people remember who they were
before the gods took pity on them?

Not everyone can be chosen to personate the gods during
our religious ceremonies. Perhaps that is why people like
me are selected to become clowns, god-mockers. The men
I killed during the Battle of the Bulge, the executions of the
SS guards at Dachau, the horror of Dachau itself so sick-
ened my spirit that, finally, only the clown society doctors
could cure me. Perhaps it is a recognition of my spirtual
strength, that I did not die from what I experienced, that
made me fit to be a clown. But once I accepted the help of
the clown society, I had no choice but to join them if I
wished to stay well.

It has not been easy being a clown. I will not say what I
have done as a clown, or whether Stephenson was wrong or
right, for religious business is religious business and not for

common knowledge. I will say that nothing I have done as a clown has been as hard to endure as seeing Dachau. And yet, I still fear to mock the gods. Where will my spirit go when I die, after I have done what I have done?

The Zuni separate men into two groups, those who are important and those who are not. To be important, a man must commission the making of a mask and wear it dancing in one of the religious ceremonies. The mask is buried when the owner dies, and then he can wear it in Kothluwalawa to dance with the gods. Clowns don't wear masks. How would I dance in Kothluwalawa?

There would have been a place for me in the old days, when warriors defended the people against raiders and oppressors. Men of courage were valued. There is no need for warriors among the Zuni any more. Our traditional enemies, the Navaho and the Hispanics, no longer threaten us. Everyone else is lumped under the term "Anglo" throughout the southwest, though the Zuni called them "Whites." Some think they are the new enemy. Men who will stand for the people against them are needed. If I am ever to be useful to my people it will have to be in this secular world. My taste of politics as bookkeeper for the tribe suggested that way, but not until I knew a lot more about the White world. It was with that faint hope that I left the Pueblo.

The job at the Fort Wingate Army Depot, outside of Gallup, opened up in August. It was during the Korean War, so the depot was loading guns and ammunition for shipment to the war front. I felt like I was back in the army, with nothing but lectures on rules and regulations for the first three days. My job description carried an indefinite temporary appointment title. If I lasted a year without being summarily fired, I would go on probationary status for two more years. They were very cautious, but no wonder. All of the administrative officers were army men.

Because of the demands from the Korean front, we worked ten hours a day, seven days a week. We were paid a dollar fifty an hour, plus time-and-a-half for overtime. The ammunition boxes weighed a hundred and ten pounds each, about half again as much as a bale of hay. I'd lifted and stacked hay bales all day long with my father, so I was able to do the work. Not everyone could. I thought they used the loading job as a way to screen out drunks and shirkers.

After two months, they took me off that job and had me blocking up the crates with braces to keep them from shifting in transit. I'd learned something about carpentry in school and could see why they needed different types of braces for different loads. The bombs were different from the ammunition boxes and the ammunition was different from the guns. The hours didn't change, though; it was still ten hours a day, seven days a week.

Commuting back and forth daily from Zuni was too hard when there wasn't even time enough to go home on weekends, so sometimes I would stay overnight at the Lexington Hotel in Gallup. It was expensive. Finally, I got an apartment with my brother Lee and my first cousin. We shared expenses and it was a lot easier. Lee was drinking too much and it worried me. I used to talk to him about it, and he always listened and said he'd try to do better, but he always went back. If we'd both stayed in Zuni during the war, it never would have happened. Most of the veterans I knew had learned to drink in the service. None of them learned to handle it.

The Korean War had been over for more than a year, but evidently no one had told Fort Wingate, so we kept on working overtime. I didn't see it as my responsibility. I'd never had any luck telling army officers anything, anyway. When the stand-down order finally came, I'd served for three years and hadn't yet gotten my permanent appointment. Fort Wingate announced a reduction in force of seven hundred employees, almost half the civilian population of the base. I thought I'd have to look for another job again. Living a white life wasn't any easier than being an Indian.

When the decision came, I found I was not one of those who had lost his job. My army service had given me a special status. I was informed that my position had been made a permanent one, with federal Civil Service status. I could stay there until I retired after thirty years of work if I wanted to. Of course, thirty years sounded like forever to me, so that didn't make much of an impression. I couldn't imagine myself being over sixty.

While waiting for the army to make up its mind, I had gone over to the Bureau of Indian Affairs office in Gallup and registered there for a job. The person who took my application was a Cherokee woman from Oklahoma, strikingly beautiful as Cherokee women are sometimes, all planes and angles. Pueblo women tend to be rounder, with softer lines. I jokingly asked her for a date, but she didn't pay any attention to me. I'd been living on my reputation as a stud without a lot of action over the past three years. It was hard to play all night and work ten hours a day, seven days a week. Even so, I'd never been flat out ignored before.

By coincidence, she was sharing an apartment with her sister right across the street from where I lived. When I saw her outside one day, I struck up a conversation and got to

know her a little bit. She said that she and her sister both
worked for the BIA and they were used to people like me
trying to pick them up. She said she'd never had one follow
her home before, though. When I said I lived at the Indian
Village, too, she was friendlier than she'd been in the office.
In time, I got her to go out with me. She took a lot of con-
vincing that I was a serious person, partly because I'd never
thought of myself that way before. When my permanent appointment came through though, I was in a position to support a wife. That was new. It became increasingly obvious
the only way I was going to get this woman was to marry
her, so I decided I'd do it. Even so, it took me a year and a
half from the time we met.

We got married in 1956 and continued to live in one of
the Indian Village apartments ten miles east of Gallup, not
far from my job. I'd drive to work in my truck and she'd
take the bus to Gallup each morning. We made our home
there for years, happily, I thought. My son, Donald, and my
daughters, Kathy and Pamela, were all born while we were
there. I learned how white people lived. We had a television
and a house full of furniture. The only language we had in
common was English, so that's what we spoke at home. Our
kids never learned anything else. My wife had been raised
this way in Tulsa, but it was a long stretch for a raggedy Indian boy, as I had once been. I remembered when my family
sat on the floor to eat supper, dipping with our fingers into
a common pot and hurrying to finish before night came. We
were happy then, too.

In a way, my Cherokee wife and I were like strangers.
We had nothing to talk about except the everyday things
that happened at the job and around us in the apartment. I
didn't know her family and she didn't know mine. Maybe

she was homesick from the first. I was, and I didn't live that far from Zuni. I was homesick for the way things used to be at Zuni, and I missed the teasing that went on all the time at home.

At work things just kept getting better for me, because I paid attention to what I was told to do, and because I didn't drink. A job opened for a carpenter and I applied, relying on the vocational training I'd taken in high school and a short stint building furniture in Albuquerque in one of those jobs that opened up for rush order work when I was first out of school. It meant a raise in wages. After five years as a carpenter, I was made maintenance foreman without even applying. The army inspectors gave me excellent ratings, which was alright with me and made my supervisor very happy. He said it reflected well on him.

New responsibilities came to me. There was a restaurant on the post and employees were asked to take turns serving as director for a year. This job was given to me and I learned to do many new things. I made out menus, ordered food supplies, and acted as personnel officer. Hiring and firing were done by the front office, but I did the interviewing. I settled disputes as they arose among the staff, and handled complaints when someone didn't like the food.

A Federal co-op credit union was formed at the Depot, enabling members to borrow money and invest their savings. The banks in Gallup weren't interested in Indian depositors and would not give Indians loans. Their excuse was that Indians could always avoid debts and foreclosures by moving their property onto the reservation. The reservation was federal land and writs from state courts didn't run there. I never understood how anyone could move a house

to the reservation, but the real estate people weren't interested in selling houses to Indians anyway.

I was selected to work on the campaign committee to en-
list employees for membership in the new credit union. Under the circumstances, it wasn't a hard job. We soon had
over a hundred members signed up with savings of over one
hundred thousand dollars we could loan out. Most loans
were for small amounts for short periods of time, and we
paid interest to the depositors from the interest we charged
for the loans. All the work was done for free and the federal
government insured the deposits, so the money was as safe
as it was in one of the Gallup banks. Safer, actually. We
were watched more closely by federal inspectors.

The next year I was on the credit union's supervisory
committee, approving loans and seeing that loans were re-
paid on schedule. I finally became the assistant treasurer,
helping the treasurer make out monthly statements, balance
sheets, and an income summary for the supervisory committee. We watched the loans and deposits so carefully that
we had almost no shortfalls.

One year, when the treasurer was on vacation, the federal inspector came through on audit and I had to handle it
all by myself. After four days, he made his report to the supervisory committee. I was shaking a little, nervous that
he'd find something wrong and I'd be held responsible. After mentioning a few unimportant discrepancies, he came to
the Treasurer's report.

"Gentlemen," he said, "it is my duty to inform you of a
shortage in the operation of the credit union stemming from
the Treasurer's office."

Everybody looked at me, and I must have appeared to be

guilty, for he said, "Mr. Wyaco, you don't have to worry." He hesitated before continuing to say, "You were only ten cents short!"

I almost fell over. Zuni tease a lot, but not like that! Everybody else laughed. I couldn't let it go, though. I said, "That's what you get for having an honest Zuni taking care of your credit union. I'm honest and I don't think there is anything I can do to have a shortage of money."

The word got around the Depot, and from then on everyone called me "Honest Zuni." I'd be walking down the street in Gallup and someone would call out to me, "Hey, Honest Zuni!" The nickname stuck to me for the rest of the time I was at the Depot. I even got to like it. It was a mark of acceptance.

This experience led me to apply for a course in army accounting at Ft. Knox, Indiana. The Equal Opportunity Act had passed Congress and all the federal institutions were looking for ways to upgrade minorities. The course lasted for three months and I spent all my time studying to keep from being lonesome. The other students were all members of minority groups, like me, Hispanics and Blacks and Navajo, and other men from other tribes of Indians. I earned a certificate of competence, which was supposed to open up an administrative position for me.

When I returned to the Depot, I became an order analyst. I would take work requests, figure out the supplies needed and the cost and man-hours involved, and order the lumber and other materials. Then I'd break down the request into its component parts and issue work orders to the various departments involved—carpentry, plumbing, electrical, or whatever was needed. When the job was completed, I'd figure if they went over or under my estimates. I was allowed a 10 percent leeway, and never exceeded it, earning a sustained excellent work rating. Once, I even got a performance award of four hundred dollars on my supervisor's recommendation. If you just looked at my behavior on the job, you would think I was turning into a first-class white man. I wanted to be able to do anything a white man could do, and do it better.

I spent more and more time at work, mastering more and more responsibilities. I became an auxiliary fireman, volunteering for duty when perhaps I should have been at home. I became the assistant property disposal officer, setting up the paperwork to declare obsolete equipment as surplus. I became the warehouse foreman because I knew where everything was. I became the Equal Employment Opportunity officer, to certify that minority employees were treated fairly. I even became the Post restaurant overseer, a position I'd held before. I was starting to repeat myself. If all of the army officers had been called to active duty someplace, I think I could have run the Depot by myself so that no one would know they were gone.

Maybe somebody above me was thinking that way, because I was sent away to Dallas to learn to be a grievance examiner, an extension of my duties as the Equal Employment Opportunity administrator. After my training, I handled four or five cases at the Depot and then was sent to Flagstaff, Arizona, to judge a case there. It was interesting. A Hispanic employee claimed he had been passed over for promotion. It took me a month to interview everyone involved and issue my findings. The Hispanic man had more seniority on the job, but the white man who was chosen over him had more relevant educational background. I ruled there was no discrimination.

While at Flagstaff, I heard about the Grand Canyon for the first time and went up to see it over a weekend. I also visited the Hopi Reservation, something I'd never done before. I was surprised at how badly the Hopi town smelled. I couldn't remember Zuni ever smelling like that.

My wife got restless with her life. It didn't change all the time like mine. She decided she wanted a house, so we applied under the G.I. Bill. We found a three bedroom house on a fifty by a hundred foot lot in a new subdivision that would be just right for us. My mother took the kids to Zuni while we settled up with the bank and the real estate people. The federal guarantee on the G.I. bill made the bank change its mind about loaning money to an Indian. We moved our furniture from the apartment, and I couldn't help thinking about how much more we had than my family had owned when I was growing up. I set up a chain-link fence in front, and enclosed the back yard with a concrete block wall, buying a swing set for the kids to play on. Over time, I planted flowers and Kentucky bluegrass, making ours the best-looking lawn on the street. Neighbors would stop and comment on it, wondering what my secret was. I'd tell them it was just hard work, but in truth I loved it.

My aunt brought the kids back to town and agreed to stay on with us as a babysitter. Four years later she remarried and left, but another Zuni woman took her place. My wife was working and the kids needed someone to be at home with them. It was good for the kids. They even started learning a little Zuni. It was good for my wife, too, not to have to do housework as soon as she came home from her job. And she had company when I was off doing one or another of the things that kept me away from home nights. But in spite of the house, she was becoming restless.

Our fourth child, a daughter, was born after we were

settled in, but my wife never said she was pregnant until my / 63
aunt noticed. Her restlessness didn't ease, and finally she
told me she wanted to leave Gallup and go back to Oklahoma. She'd thought it all out. She wanted me to withdraw
my federal job retirement money and go into some kind of
business back there.

She was just being Cherokee. She told me once, in the
old days the highest honor a Cherokee could win was to
steal a tethered horse from in back of an enemy's teepee. I'd
said it sounded risky to me. She'd replied that that was the
point: the honor depended on the risk.

Zuni are different. They're brave enough. In the old days,
they'd hunted bears with a bow and arrow. I knew I could
face any danger a Cherokee could. I'd proved it. It was different with Cherokee, though. They sought out danger. She
couldn't see why I didn't jump at the chance to win big by
taking a big risk. I had all the skills to succeed in business after my experience at the Depot.

What I couldn't tell her was that living with her had made
me a better Zuni than I had ever started out to be. I'd
learned to be patient like a real Zuni man. Zuni women did
what they wanted to at home. Men were just guests in their
wives' houses. The children belong to them, clan members
by birth. I'd never argued with my wife. (Of course, you
can't argue with a Cherokee, anyway. You can fight, but you
can't argue. But I didn't do that, either.) I tried to explain
my reluctance to leave the Depot, giving the example of a
man who had to return to work at the Depot after he lost all
of his retirement money after just two years in an unsuc-
cessful business. He was lucky there was a job waiting for
him. If I left, there would be no job later waiting for me.
There was talk of further reductions in force at the Depot.

Then she said she'd withdraw her money, too, and I

didn't give her any kind of answer on that. That's when she got mad. In the summer of 1968 she took the kids back to Oklahoma with her. It didn't occur to me that she might not return. She took only the kids and their clothes. Even so, I was thinking like a Zuni. Children belong to their mothers.

I stayed on at the Depot and worked, going to Oklahoma twice that summer to see my family and to try to talk her into coming back. The children wanted to. All their friends were in New Mexico. She wouldn't do it, though, and I didn't ask her to come back again, waiting instead for her to make up her mind. That fall, she filed for divorce in Tulsa.

She wrote me, along with her lawyer, asking me to agree to the property division and to supply child support until the kids turned eighteen. I went to a lawyer myself and showed him the papers. There was no child support specified, so he asked me what my salary was. Then he advised me to offer a hundred dollars a month per child. That was all right with me. I could pay that without hurting too much in case I got married again. I'm not the kind of man who should live by himself.

I kept the house in Gallup, and she kept property she'd inherited in Oklahoma. I sent her all the furniture except a couch to sleep on, a rocker, a table and two chairs, and the television. I'd come home and sit in the rocker and rock and watch the TV until I went to sleep. I'd never been so lonesome in my life.

CHAPTER 7

When I was making my last, sad visit to Tulsa, I read a notice in the newspaper that applications were being accepted for jobs in the post office. I had the idea at the time that I might be able to take a job in Tulsa and be with my family, so I went down to the post office and applied. I was asked if I wanted to be a clerk, a mail handler, or a postmaster and told to come back in two days for appropriate testing.

"Why not shoot for the top?" I thought. I sounded like a Comanche. They said the government service rate for postmaster was GS-11, four steps up from the GS-7 rate I then held. It meant more money. Sounded good to me.

On test day, I reported in at eight in the morning and answered questions until almost noon. It was like a test I'd taken for supervisor back at Fort Wingate. The first part was memory testing, seeing how well you could recall lists of street numbers, telephone numbers, and road names. You got to study half a page of information for ten minutes and then put down what you could remember of it in the rest of the hour. It was easy. Zuni boys are trained to recite long, complicated prayers and stories word for word.

There were other tests, on how fast you could spot numbers and put them in boxes, and on basic math and English comprehension. There was a life history form to fill out, particularly covering educational and job experience. I didn't think any more about it and heard nothing for two months. When the letter on the test results came, I was back in Gallup. I set it aside, not interested in it any longer because, by that time, it was obvious to me that my marriage was over. Why would I want a job in Tulsa?

A week later, out of curiosity more than anything else, I opened it and found I'd passed the test. I was surprised but happy because the Depot was going through another reduction in force, down to eighty-eight employees. I'd received a letter from the Army saying I was scheduled to be released from my employment even before I'd visited Tulsa. The letter from the post office said I was eligible to be a postmaster anywhere, even Gallup. I hadn't liked the idea of looking for work again. I was forty-five, with house payments and child support to keep up. My children called me every month when I sent the money for them, and I didn't want to be cut completely off. Furthermore, I'd lose my house like I'd lost my family if my job stopped. I hadn't worked quite long enough to retire, even counting my army time.

I told the Depot people about the post office job possibility and they told me they'd decided not to terminate me after all. For ten years I'd served on the volunteer fire department, and I'd taken special training with professional fire departments, which now qualified me for a permanent firefighter's position. I'd have to take a cut in pay, I was told, but I could stay on at the Depot until I was eligible for retirement if I wanted to. Actually, it turned out that, as a firefighter on base twenty-four hours a day I was able to get extra money, so the move from management to firefighting didn't cost me anything. It was just one more experience in the white world, one that I couldn't have had if I were still married.

Some of those whose jobs were cut found similar jobs in
the Bureau of Indian Affairs at Gallup, but most had to go to
Colorado to find work. I was lucky.

I don't know what I would have done if I had continued
just living by myself and being a firefighter. The hours I was
expected to keep were so irregular, I couldn't even think of
getting married again. I sometimes would work three days
on call for twenty-four hours and then be off five days, then
work again for four days, on a twenty-four hour on-call
shift. I couldn't go home when I was on duty. No woman
was going to stand for that.

Fortunately for me, as it turned out, Zuni had passed a
new, formal constitution in 1970. This was the latest move
in what was a long battle between the old religious hierarchy at Zuni and the white outside world. When the Spanish
owned New Mexico, they refused to deal with the Zuni religious leaders, who they called "diabolists." Instead, they
insisted that secular officers be appointed, much like those
found in Spanish villages. So the Zuni religious leaders
obliged and appointed such people, although keeping a very
tight rein on their actions. The religious leaders even came
to prefer this system, since it placed a buffer between them
and the Spanish outsiders. Dealing with the Spaniards was
always a chancy activity because of the clash of cultures, and
besides, Zuni religious practices required an atmosphere of
peace and calm.

This system was still in place when the United States
took the land from Mexico in 1848. At various times, army
officers and/or Christian missionaries tried to make themselves the Zuni's representatives in the outside world, but
they found they still had to deal with the Zuni secular officers selected by the religious leaders, an unsatisfactory arrangement from their point of view. Things changed during

the New Deal of the 1930s, when John Collier was appointed Commissioner of Indian Affairs. Collier had been a field worker for the National Council of Women's Clubs, a powerful group that had become interested in the condition of Indian women and children. The president of this group was Mrs. Harold Ickes. When Ickes became Secretary of the Interior, the cabinet officer responsible for the Bureau of Indian Affairs, Collier's appointment became inevitable.

Collier was a visionary, much admired by Whites and reviled by Indians, even today, but his appointees and his innovations in the administration of Indian affairs changed Indian life forever. The government became more intrusive in Indian affairs than even the Spanish had tried to be. Collier's agent for the United Pueblos BIA office in Albuquerque was a woman named Sophie Aberle. Aberle found that at Zuni each time she tried to institute a Collier reform through the pueblo governor and his council, the religious hierarchy would remove these officers from power. Exasperated by her inability to implement new policies, Aberle declared that the religious hierarchy would no longer have any authority over secular officers. If some officious federal employee tried that today, she would find herself in court, but in 1941 Indians didn't realize they had civil rights.

Thereafter, the Zuni chose their Governor, Lieutenant Governor, and six council members from among those who announced they wanted to run for office. The candidates would come before the people in a general assembly, and the people would stand and vote by a show of hands, with the man having the most support becoming Governor, the next becoming Lieutenant Governor, and on down the line until six councilmen were chosen as well. This worked all right, but it wasn't a Zuni way of doing things. In fact,

the only reason it worked at all was because the religious / 69
leaders told certain individuals they had to put themselves
forward. The Zuni have always been suspicious of anyone
who decides on such things himself.

When I was a boy, no one wanted to be Governor because it took time away from the fields and carried no salary.
The Rain Priest of the North, the highest religious person in
the pueblo, would come to a man's house and inform him
of his having been selected. No one would argue with the
priest. Only someone with a bad heart would argue with a
man so holy. Of course, the would-be officeholder might
plead incompetence. It never did any good, but it showed
a commendable distaste for power, a very Zuni kind of
feeling.

There was little for a governor to do, since the tribe had
no budget. Later on, there were federally funded programs
to run and the job became more interesting. When I was
bookkeeper for the tribe for three years, after I came back
from service, the transition had already started.

The Constitution that was approved in 1970 was the result of three years' work using funds provided by the Indian
Reorganization Act, one of John Collier's most far-reaching
pieces of legislation. Collier thought all Indians should have
democratic government, with checks and balances and au-
dits on the expenditure of funds. At Zuni, there were always quarrels about the spending of tribal money, so most
Zuni thought this would be a good thing: men could run for
office without scandal attached to their names at the ends of
their terms. Everything would be out in the open.

The new Zuni Constitution provided for four-year terms
for tribal officers, who would now be elected by secret bal-
lot. All during the time I lived in Gallup, I'd been attending

the general assemblies when I could, out of general interest. I'd never lost sight of my dream to be of use to the people in some capacity. Sometimes I would speak in the assembly, and perhaps it was noticed that I had constructive ideas. One day, a highly respected Zuni man came to me in Gallup and asked me to permit my name to be submitted for councilman under the new Constitution. He wasn't the sort of person I could argue with.

The Superintendent of the United Pueblo Office of the Bureau of Indian Affairs in Albuquerque called me to find out if I were serious about running, since I was still working at the Army Depot at Fort Wingate. The way our work time was arranged, I knew I could always get off to attend an evening meeting and told him so. When the official ballots were printed, there my name was. I was only forty-six years old, younger than any of the other eleven men running. I didn't think I had a change to be elected.

I didn't even go to Zuni on election day to vote. I thought maybe it would show I was too eager. They counted the votes for Governor and Lieutenant Governor and announced them on the radio as totals came in. There was no mention of the councilman races.

About ten-thirty I got sleepy and turned the radio off, sure I was too young to be considered seriously. Then, about four in the morning, Mr. Robert Lewis called from Zuni to say I'd been elected to the Council—but there was a problem. Another man and I were leading all the other candidates, but we had each received the same number of votes. The person with the most votes was to be named head councilman, or Head Teniente, a designation derived from the Spanish. The person with the second highest number of votes would be designated Second Teniente, and the rest were just councilmen.

I offered to take second place because the other man was older, but Mr. Lewis said that wouldn't be fair to all those who had voted for me. So I suggested flipping a coin. I said I'd take tails. The chairman of the election committee agreed to do it and the coin came up tails. I was named Head Teniente.

I went back to bed thinking, "Oh, gosh, what have I got myself into? I'm still working . . . I've never been on the Council before. I don't know how to lead the people." I even thought about withdrawing or resigning in sheer panic. Finally, I decided that the people who had voted for me would think, "Why did he run anyway? He's just a quitter. Why did he have to go through all that and quit? We got him elected and he broke faith with us. He doesn't want to be a leader and do a good job for the people." I did, though.

When dawn came, I hadn't slept at all, but I had made up my mind. I was going to accept and do the best I could. The next day I asked for leave and went down to Zuni and met the new governing body. I knew who they all were because they were older than me, but I didn't know any of them well. It embarrassed me to be the head man. I just waited while the others arranged to have the oath given.

The inauguration was held in the plaza, the sacred place in the middle of the village. The masked dances are held there, too. I was given a cane of office, not the Lincoln cane, but another one. The Lincoln cane goes to the Governor. Abraham Lincoln gave each of the pueblos a black, silver-headed cane of office when he was president.

I took my cane back to the council office and found my mother and uncle there waiting for me. My mother was crying, all upset. I asked her why. I had thought she would be proud of me.

"Being in politics is a hard life," she said. She'd cry and

then say a few words, then cry and speak again. "You've never experienced any criticism before . . . You don't know what it's like . . . You'll be chopped down . . . People will call you all kinds of names . . . They may not even respect you later on . . . I wish you'd never run for the Council . . . I'm crying because I feel sorry for you."

My uncle, who had served on the council, said: "It won't be so bad. I don't think there will be any real problems. You just have to get used to it. You know you can't satisfy all the people all the time anyway, no matter what you do. There will be all kinds of criticism. There always is. As long as the other council members don't care, Virgil shouldn't either. Just don't pay any attention to all the rumors. Just let them go in one ear and out the other. That way it won't be too hard on you when you carry out your duties on the council."

I knew how rumors went. I'd learned not to pay any attention to them in the army. It was the same at the Depot. There were always people who seemed to know everything before it actually happened. Most of the time, it never did.

The first day of business was January 2, 1971. We spent it in orientation, stating what we wanted to do as individual office holders and listening to what the others felt should be done. We set our priorities, talking about what had been done in the past, what projects were in the middle of completion, and what should be done in the future. The Superintendent of the United Pueblo Office of the BIA attended, along with his legal services representative, and told us what monies were available to us to fund the operations we planned. The new governor ran the meeting, which took a lot of pressure off me. I was afraid I'd have to do it.

On the second day, the governor appointed me to head

the Zuni Education Department and to act as liaison between the Zuni Housing Authority and the federal government. There were negotiations going on to build federally
financed low-cost housing in Zuni. Neither of these duties
required constant meetings, so I was able to handle them
and continue doing my job at the same time. I was finally
doing what I dreamed of doing all of my life: being useful to
my people.

I stayed at the Depot until January of 1972, when the
postmaster at Zuni put in for retirement, and I was notified
of my eligibility for the job. There was a federal policy to
hire minority workers when possible. There was another
Zuni working in the post office at Gallup who was offered
the job first. It would have been a promotion for him, but he
wanted to continue to live in Gallup and the commute
thirty miles each way to Zuni, particularly in the winter
time, discouraged him.

The Gallup postmaster, who had the responsibility for
making the appointment, asked me if I wanted the job and
took my application, including more forms I had to fill out.
It was weeks before he told me I was approved and could
start immediately. The good part was that I could transfer
my federal retirement pension to my new job.

I gave the Depot people two weeks' notice and reported
for work on April 10th of 1972, knowing absolutely nothing
about what I was supposed to do. There was a clerk on duty
at Zuni who could teach me my job, along with manuals that
spelled everything out as far as rules and regulations went.
I'd been reading technical manuals ever since I first started
at Fort Wingate, so that didn't bother me. By the end of the
first day, I had some idea of what was expected, by the end
of the second month I knew the job, and by the end of that

year I had gone to San Francisco for the final interview and had been given permanent status as postmaster. Because everything takes more time than it should when you're dealing with the federal government, the official notice was dated August 4, 1973. I'd done it. I'd found a white man's job in my own home pueblo. Maybe now I could start thinking like an Indian again.

I came to know everyone in Zuni by name at the post office. I'd been gone most of the time for twenty-five years, and I didn't even always recognize people I'd known as a boy. With the young people growing up, it was impossible, but I was soon on a first-name basis with everyone in town, all the adults, anyway. I teased almost everyone. Some people took themselves more seriously than they should and didn't always appreciate it.

"Why isn't my magazine here? It usually comes in today," someone would demand.

"I'm a slow reader," I'd say. "I haven't finished with it yet." I suppose if complaints would have been sent into the post office in Gallup, I'd have heard about it, but no one every carried it that far.

Sometimes people would say, "I want this to go the fastest, cheapest way," and I'd have to explain there was no fastest, cheapest way. There were cheap, slow ways and fast, expensive ways. I couldn't haggle. The post office rates are fixed, but some people didn't understand that. They thought I could if I wanted to, and accused me of doing it for others. I could keep my temper through that, and even when some old person accused me of stealing a Social Security check. Old people are sometimes cross because they don't feel well, or because they hate living all alone. I did have trouble being pleasant to some of the non-Zunis who expected to

have their mail forwarded all the time without paying post-
age due charges. Sometimes, I was pretty short with them.

One more thing happened to me when I returned to Zuni that gave me the anchor I'd always needed in my life. I met and married a young widow, a traditional Zuni woman who has made me very happy. She is a very private person who doesn't want to be talked about, so I won't. For myself, I will say it was the best thing I ever did.

CHAPTER 8

I became a public man. This has a special meaning in Zuni. Someone did a study of irrational fears people have in the white world. The one held by the most Whites is the fear of public speaking. It's like that for the Zuni, only worse: among the Zuni, it's not an irrational fear, and speaking in public is only part of it. Someone who is a public man becomes one knowing that he will become a target for gossip, envy, and spite. A public man knows that some people become so eaten up by evil thoughts about public men that they become witches and use witch power to injure them if they can. Public men become vulnerable to witch attack if they use their power to act for themselves rather than for the good of all.

I was very careful, for I knew drawing attention to yourself was dangerous, but I was not afraid. First, half the people I knew outside of the pueblo called me "Honest Zuni." If I could build a reputation like that in the White world, I should be able to do it at home. Second, I wasn't afraid of just talk. I'd lived through a time when people were shooting at me and trying to kill me. And third, I didn't take myself too seriously. It helped me to keep things in perspective when people would come up to me and say, "I voted for you."

"Well, thank you," I'd say, "But, why did you do

that?" thinking they'd answer it was because I was young
like them, or good-looking, or spoke well at the general
assemblies.

"Oh," they'd say, "I didn't even know who you were. I
just liked the name, Virgil." It was hard to think of myself
too seriously when I heard that kind of thing.

I had a lot to learn during my first terms as councilman.
The older men taught me my job. There are ways of con-
ducting a meeting as a Zuni that I had to learn. I may have
had more formal education than the others, but I knew less
about being a Zuni than any of them. I knew some things, of
course. For instance, the Zuni let whoever is speaking come
to the end of what he wants to say without interrupting.
White people seem to interrupt each other all the time in
conversation. They seem not to be interested in any opinion
but their own. The Zuni think it is more fair to hear all sides
of a question, and it saves time as well. If people know their
opinion has been heard, they don't make so much of a fuss
when a decision goes against them.

As the council's contact man for education, I was sent to
the meetings of the Southwestern Indian Polytechnic Institute in Albuquerque. SIPI, as it was called, had been organized in 1969 or 1970, and that first year the Zuni Chief of
Police had attended meetings of the board because no one
else wanted to.

When I came on the SIPI board in 1971, a Navajo, Mar-
shall Tomé, was chairman. Most of the other board members were from the pueblos: Santo Domingo, San Felipe,
San Juan, Isleta, Santa Clara, Acoma, Laguna and me, repre-
senting the Zuni. Other members came from the Sioux,
Mescalero Apache, Jicarilla Apache from Dulce in New
Mexico, and Pima from Arizona.

There were elections held each year among the SIPI board members, and in 1973 I was made vice-chairman, a surprise to me after one short year as a member. In 1974 the Mescalero representative, Evelyn Bruinger, nominated me for chairman and I was elected to that office. I don't know what I did to earn such confidence from the other board members, but I was proud of it. These weren't just Zuni choosing one of their own.

The tribe decided to establish its own school district that same year, rather than stay under the McKinley County school district. Zuni parents wanted more of a say in what their children were taught, and most of the McKinley County board was made up of Whites. Not all, though. I was chairman of that board, too. We had to have the permission of the county board to ask the state for a new district, and then we had to go through the state legislature for approval. The Zuni gave me credit for bringing that about. I brought Johnson–O'Malley funds from the old county district to the new school district. These are federal impact funds given to school districts with sizable numbers of Indian school children to educate. Indian reservation lands are not subject to state taxes, and state taxes support public schools. The Johnson-O'Malley money is supposed to reimburse the state for the cost of educating Indian children. I was also asked to be a member of the new Zuni school district, but I was getting too busy with all the community service and had to turn it down.

This all happened in my final year on the tribal council. People urged me to run for a second term on the council, so I put my name in again. I was the only council member to be returned for a second term. When the others were replaced, I thought sure I would be as well, since I was so identified with the council by that time. Maybe people still liked my name.

Since I stayed on the council, I also stayed on the SIPI board and was made chairman for each of the next four years. I would probably have remained on the SIPI board even if I hadn't run for the council because I was sitting as chairman. As it was, I stayed chairman for the total time of my new term, and beyond. I could have stayed forever, maybe, as far as SIPI was concerned, because I saved it from the Secretary of Interior, James Watt, who wanted to close it down.

In 1976 we learned from the newspaper that Secretary Watt, with the concurrence of the Bureau of Indian Affairs Commissioner, Ken Smith, had decided that SIPI should be closed to save money. From the newspaper! Secretary Watt thought any time you kept Congress from spending money, it was a good thing, at least for the big taxpayers who objected to seeing the money they earned taxed away and spent on anyone else. No one had told the SIPI board anything about the decision in advance.

The board confronted the Department of Interior and the BIA and was told that the newspaper reports were correct. We asked what their justification for such high-handed measures might be, and they said that SIPI duplicated other services. They said any Indians who wanted vocational education could go to Albuquerque's Technical Vocational Institute. Any SIPI student who wanted to continue with specialized Indian training could go to the Haskell Indian School in Lawrence, Kansas. They said there was nothing to discuss, the decision had been made.

The longer this went on, the more I could feel myself becoming angry. I know better than to lose my temper. I went through the Battle of the Bulge without getting angry, using corn meal to pray every day for calm. I was numb with cold much of the time, jumpy from the constant noise, dopey from lack of sleep and frightened from getting shot at, but I didn't get angry until I saw Dachau. It got into my head so deeply that ten years later I had to have the clown society doctor take it out.

What James Watt and Ken Smith were doing was just a continuation of the kind of thing I'd run into all of my life. When I was a little boy, I'd heard White teachers call Indian children dirty and stupid because we couldn't speak English well and wore ragged clothes. I never said that I spoke Zuni fluently, which is a more poetic language than English, and that I bathed more often than they did, but it was true enough. White teachers had called me a thief for roasting corn that was intended to feed the hogs. They fed the hogs better than they fed the students. When they drafted me, I was expected to serve like everybody else, but I couldn't vote because I was an Indian. When I got out, I couldn't have a beer with my friends in college because it was against the law to serve Indians liquor. I had to have a G.I. loan backed by the government before the bank in Gallup would consider helping me to finance the purchase of a house, because I was an Indian.

I thought I was used to this kind of treatment after all this time. What James Watt and Ken Smith did was humiliating, though. And this time, it wasn't just happening to me. If I let them close SIPI when I was chairman of the SIPI board, it would be like saying to all of the students that they didn't count for anything because they were Indians. I knew that not consulting us before taking the decision was not done in ignorance. They knew we wouldn't like it. They didn't care, because they thought it didn't matter how we felt. The other members of the board agreed with me, and we decided to fight.

Our legal advisor, Mr. Robert Bennett, told us that closing SIPI was a violation of the Indian Education Act. We had legal grounds for protest. The board and all the tribes that supported SIPI should have been consulted. It was the law. Mr. Bennett advised us to file a suit to get an injunction against the Secretary's action. It would cost about $50,000 to carry it through, but the BIA would probably have to pay it in the end, since they were party to the wrongdoing.

He told us that waiting for a legal decision would take so much time that SIPI would be closed before the matter could be addressed, so he advised us to lobby our congressmen and senators for help. He said he doubted if they could do anything, since most of the western lawmakers were angry at James Watt for one thing or another anyway, and Watt didn't pay any attention to them. He said the Secretary's order had already been given, and judging by past events, he wasn't going to take it back because someone in Congress asked him to.

Our first step was to file the suit against the Interior Department and the BIA. We went to the All-Pueblo Indian Council for help, asking them to go along with us in a joint complaint, but the chairman, Del Lovato, said no. He said he agreed with James Watt. We should have known better. Under Lovato, the AIPC just echoed whatever the BIA wanted. Lovato said he thought it was alright to close SIPI and send the Indian students to Albuquerque's Technical Vocational Institute or to the Haskell Indian School in Kansas. We were on our own.

Mr. Bennett recommended that we hire Richard Hughes

as our attorney. Our suit delayed the execution of the Secretary's order, but we couldn't leave it there. Mr. Hughes told us that the courts were very reluctant to get into the area of administrative law, even when it is clear that something is wrong. When the Senate Committee on the Interior decided to hold a hearing on the matter, in March of 1978, the SIPI board decided to send three of us to Washington to attend. I was chosen to go, along with a man from Cochiti Pueblo, who was the board's vice-chairman, and one of the students, who headed the SIPI student body. Since it was the students who would be most affected by the closure, we thought they should have a voice in defending its staying open.

We held a meeting at the Sheraton Hotel in Albuquerque to announce our plans and gain support. As speakers, we had Wendell Chino from the Mescalero Apache, Peter McDonald from the Navajo, Robert Lewis from Zuni, and Dave Warren from Santa Clara, all tribal chairmen or pueblo governors. We got the head of every tribe with students at SIPI to write a letter of support. We took the letters with us to Washington, knowing we had the backing of our Indian people.

Senator Mark Andrews opened the hearing at nine o'clock. The first man to testify was Del Lavato, chairman of the All-Indian Pueblo Council. He said he didn't think closing SIPI would interrupt the education of the Indian students enrolled there. He said that they could get as good an education at the Albuquerque Technical Vocational Institute or at the Haskell Indian School. After he was through giving his prepared statement, which sounded as if someone had written it for him, some of the committee members asked him questions. He didn't have very good answers. He wasn't speaking from the heart.

Ken Smith spoke next for the Department of the Interior. He said that enrollment at the school was down and that serious students avoided attending the school because, he said, the quality of education was poor and students who did attend spent their time drinking and partying. He said it was impossible to study at night because of unauthorized persons going in and out of the dormitories at all hours. He made SIPI sound more like a honky-tonk bar than a school.

Senator Andrews was very sharp with Ken Smith, I don't know why. I had the feeling Ken Smith had given unsatisfactory testimony to the committee before. The Senator was interested in facts, not impressions and asked questions for specific numbers. Ken Smith couldn't answer the questions, saying he'd have to research them and send in answers later. He didn't seem to know anything specific; in fact, he knew so little that I was embarrassed for him.

Very few lights were on in the hearing room until my testimony was announced. Suddenly there was a big stir in the room, the lights came on, and the TV cameras were focused on me. I was surprised, but I put that out of my mind. I didn't need to read some statement made up by some lawyer. I knew why SIPI should stay open.

First, I said Ken Smith was wrong about the enrollment figures at SIPI. I said that when I first joined the board, there were 250 students. I'd been on the board for eight years and its chairman for six. During that time, enrollment at SIPI had doubled. I told them that eight years ago, along with other board members, I had talked to students and teachers to find out if there were problems that the board could help solve. We heard then that there were problems of the sort Ken Smith had described, but we also heard that the students themselves were committed to solving these problems and not allowing them to continue. We had asked the president of the student body to work out a student code with the other students and bring it to us. They did. It was very strict. We approved it, and since that time the problems Ken Smith talked about had disappeared.

I told the committee that it was illegal to close SIPI since it had been opened under the Indian Education Act. I told them we had no objection to the Haskell Institute in principle. It is a very fine school; Haskell graduates have always been proud of having gone there, and many of them have become successful in the white world. But, I said, it wasn't easy for Pueblo Indian students to attend Haskell because our religion demands the participation of pueblo members many times throughout the year. I said that Lawrence, Kansas, where Haskell is located is too far from home for Pueblo young people with religious obligations. I said the Albuquerque Technical Vocational Institute also had good programs, but that they were designed for a walk-in student body. They had no dormitories. Some Indians do go there part-time, holding down regular jobs in town, but they are older, for the most part, than SIPI's students, and self-sufficient financially.

I said SIPI is a different kind of school, designed for young, full-time students but with enough flexibility that time could be taken for required home visits without penalty. I read a few lines from some of the letters of endorsement the pueblo governors had given me.

I explained that all the letters stressed the importance of education to Indians. Like other minority groups, Indians need education to survive in a world dominated by Whites. I pointed out that millions of dollars had been spent on SIPI already and that its physical plant, its buildings and equipment, were brand new. What would be saved if the same

students were put on scholarships some place else? I said it
was just because SIPI was for Indians that Secretary Watt decided to close it down. He didn't think Indians deserved any
kind of special treatment, and he was willing to break the
law passed by Congress, the Indian Reorganization Act, to
make his point.

There were questions afterwards, which I handled better
than any of the others who testified. The difference was, I
knew what I was talking about and they didn't, at least not
in detail. Ken Smith must have been relying on a report ten
years old for his information. He was pathetic.

Following my testimony, I found reporters in the hall
waiting to talk to me. They asked a lot of questions, mostly
about Zuni. I had the feeling some of them had never talked
to a real, live Indian before. It was like being in a zoo. Afterwards, we were taken to see some senators and congressmen. We met Senator Edward Kennedy and Senator Pete
Domenici. They both said they were on our side in the dis-
pute. Even though Senator Domenici is a Republican, he
didn't seem to like James Watt any better than Senator
Kennedy did. Our New Mexico congressmen were Mike
Runnels and "Little Joe" Montoya, and they both said we
could count on them to do what they could. Congressman
Montoya sent us to see Sidney Yates, a congressman from
Chicago, who was head of the House Committee on Indian
Affairs.

I wondered why a congressman from Chicago would be
interested in Indians, but he told me his district included
Uptown, a neighborhood in the city where thousands of reservation Indians, mostly Sioux and Chippewa, had come to
live. He said the conditions under which urban Indians live
are terrible, worse than the poorest of reservations, where

there are at least some social services available. He promised to include funds for SIPI in the federal budget, no matter what James Watt wanted.

We went to the BIA to call on Ken Smith, as a courtesy. He said my testimony had been very strong, but it was respectful. He was right. I hadn't called him a liar or anything like that. If I had been a BIA employee, I'd have been fired for disagreeing with him, but he had no hold on me. I wondered what hold he had on Del Lovato.

When we got back from Washington, people in Zuni kept telling me they'd seen me on television. I may have been the first Zuni that ever happened to. One shot showed me getting off the plane at Albuquerque, and some of the people were calling me a movie star. They wanted to know when I would be acting again. Zuni do a lot of teasing. With all the talk, the funny part was I never did get to see myself on television. I can't say for sure how I looked.

We thought it was over, but on May 19th all the employees of SIPI got their termination papers. I was down at the Zuni council offices and received a call from Mr. Martin, the president of SIPI. He said the staff had been told they had until June 30 to find new employment. He said the teachers were asking him about annual leave time, severance pay, job counseling, or whatever other services might be available.

I called Congressman Sidney Yates in Washington and told him about it because he had assured us SIPI would stay open. He said to get back to Mr. Martin and tell him to tear up the termination papers. The congressman said he was going to call James Watt and Ken Smith personally and tell them he was authorizing a supplemental appropriation to keep SIPI open. So, I called Mr. Martin back and told him to

file the termination forms in the wastebasket. SIPI was going to stay alive. I was a hero at SIPI. Mr. Yates saved SIPI,
but I got all the credit. That may have been the first time in
history an Indian got credit for something good that a white
man was responsible for, instead of the other way around.

I decided not to run for the Zuni Council again. I'd spent
so much time away from my job at the post office that my
supervisor in Farmington hinted I could be in trouble. I
wondered if his attitude wasn't a result of a payback call
from James Watt or Ken Smith to some politician high up in
the postal service, but I never asked. I stayed on with SIPI,
though. Everybody thought I ought to watch over it for a
while, so I did for a few years. It was in fine shape when I
left the board and is still in operation. I'm happy I had something to do with it.

CHAPTER 9

*F*or a few years after my second term on the Council expired in 1978 I was out of public life, content with having done my duty by the pueblo. I just watched but what I saw was distressing. The new governor that had been elected died in June, 1979. The constitution provided for the lieutenant governor. The vacancy for first teniente would be filled by a special election. Well, they didn't do that. They moved the second teniente to the lieutenant governor's seat, passing over the first teniente, eliminating any need to go back to the people. It was pointed out to them at several general assemblies that they had gone against the constitution, but the new governor and the council all said the constitution was ambiguous and that they could do what they wanted to. They had gotten sick with power, always a danger for men in public life.

I was glad I wasn't on the council this time. I'd have been fighting with them most of the time, for what they did was wrong. Imagine, defying the people! Some people were mad at me anyway, saying it never would have happened if I'd been there to stop it. They were right, but I just thought, "Haven't I served enough?" Power had no hold on me. I didn't crave office just to have it. That's why witches had been unable to harm me all those years. I know there had been some who tried.

The old men, the religious leaders of the pueblo, came
by the homes of the new governor and the whole council,
taking away their canes of office, like in the old days. The
officers could not refuse to surrender their canes. The religious leaders were the rightful custodians of them. The governor and the council could refuse to step down, though,
and did, since they'd been elected under the constitution instead of just appointed.

Some people started a recall petition to remove them, an
action possible under the constitution, but all that accom-
plished was to split the pueblo into two groups, those who
thought the elected officials should serve out their terms
and those who thought they should resign. Nothing was resolved, but no one in either faction respected them. Their
relatives were ashamed, even if they had to stand by them.

Efforts were made to involve the BIA in the quarrel. The
BIA had always been willing to interfere in Zuni business before. This time they just said there was nothing they could
do until finally the superintendent, Mr. Montgomery, sent a
memo stating that the Council and governor should abide
by the constitution and hold an election to name a new first
teniente. Shortly after, the BIA transferred Mr. Montgomery. The governor and council bragged they had been responsible, using their influence to get him out. Maybe, but
some people thought it was my fault that the BIA didn't back
Mr. Montgomery. They said the BIA may have decided not
to mess with Zuni tribal affairs anymore after I made them
back down over the closure of SIPI. Under other circumstances, I might have been proud of it.

The religious leaders came to me and asked me to run for
governor when the time came for new elections to help restore respect for the tribal government. I was still working

at the post office and knew I'd have to retire if I won that office. The old men insisted anyhow and almost convinced me but on the last day to file I got cold feet and declared for the council again instead. I promised I'd run for governor some time after I retired. I was elected to the Council and went back to being the contact man for education and housing. I was also appointed liaison for the Senior Citizen Center since I was a senior citizen myself now. And a new responsibility came to me: I was named tribal treasurer. It was the first time there had been such a position at Zuni, but it was also the first time there was any considerable amount of money to look after. People remembered how I had kept books for the tribe years ago. Old "Honest Zuni" was back.

One of my first problems as treasurer was to decide what to do about our Indian land claims suit against the federal government. When I first became a councilman in 1971 I'd learned about the Indian Land Claims Act that the congress had passed to permit tribes to sue for the illegal taking of tribal lands. The act set up a special commission to hear the claims. It looked simple on paper then until the lawyers got into it. The act said all claims were to be settled by 1961 but the time had to be extended again and again because lawyers on both sides stretched things out.

One problem was that there didn't seem to be a body of law spelling out what Indian rights to the land were. Some nineteenth century rulings of the United States Supreme Court held that Indian title was something different than title held by Whites. They held that Indian title was based on use rights rather than ownership rights and there were no standards under White law to judge what use rights were worth.

What Indians have always felt about their relationship to

their lands played right into this thinking. Indians don't believe land is owned by men. In fact, there are some who feel
that the land owns them. When they made treaties back a
hundred years ago or more, giving away huge tracts of land
for almost nothing, they were just inviting Whites to share
the land with them. It's hard to prove now because the
treaty records were kept by Whites. Nevertheless, Indians
have word-of-mouth recollections which show what they
meant.

If Indians then felt as we Zuni do now, they considered
the land to be holy, somewhat in the way a White man
might think of a church graveyard as holy where his parents
were buried. Would even a White man sell such a place?
Whites don't seem to understand that Indians feel about all
of the land given them by the gods the way the Whites feel
about graveyards.

I was on the Council the first time when the two lawyers
from Utah, E. Richard Hart and Steve Boyden, filed suit for
the Zuni before the Indian Claims Commission. Most of
the Zuni thought we were suing to get our land back even
though the Commission had power only to make money
judgments. It's hard to distinguish between the concepts,
"to restore lands taken," and "to make restitution for lands
taken" in the Zuni language when the idea of selling the land
given the Zuni by the gods is impossible to consider in the
first place. Some of our old men didn't speak English.

The good part was that in the Zuni hearings, the Commission listened politely to the old men as they related the
traditional stories about the Zuni land. The Commission re-
lied on the testimony of archaeologists, historians, and land
evaluators to make their decision, however, so the old men's
day in court was just for show. The respect wasn't real.

I don't say the lawyers lied, but they didn't try very hard to make it clear to the old men who cared the most about it that a return of the lands couldn't be done. I don't understand it myself. Much of the land claimed lies in what is now the Cibola National Forest. It has never had fee simple title issued on it to individual owners. Why couldn't the federal government just give it back to the tribe?

Did the Zuni benefit from all of this legal maneuvering? It's hard to see how. We can't spend the money without approval of the BIA. The BIA is the arm of government that ruined our lands in the first place, and is our contact with the same government who took the lands they would now pay for. Before the awards, capital expenditures for improvements on the reservation would have come out of federal general funds. Now the government wants us to spend our own money.

If I had it to do over again, I think I would become a lawyer. I can understand any book on accounting. I've worked under post office rules and regulations that few people beside the ones who wrote them truly understand. I've even read army manuals on the care and maintenance of heavy equipment and kept the equipment in working order though nobody understands army manuals. How much harder would it be to read law books? A lawyer could defend the tribe in much the same way as an old time warrior defended it against its enemies.

In recent history Indians have been considered wards of the federal government and those rights have been guarded, supposedly, by the Bureau of Indian Affairs. Everyone is familiar with the stereotype of the villainous Indian agent to be found in cowboy movies. This is about as far from the real historical facts as the way Indians are portrayed. There

were good agents and bad agents like there are other good
and bad men everywhere, even now. What is becoming
clear, however, is that the BIA as an institution has become
increasingly ineffective as a guardian of Indian rights. Most
shocking have been recent revelations of mismanagement of
Indian trust funds. There may be tens, even hundreds of
millions of dollars lost to Indian tribes through poor and
even criminal negligence.

I retired from the post office at about
the same time I finished my term as
councilman. The federal pension that seemed so unimportant forty years ago makes my life comfortable now. Things
I looked forward to doing for years now fill my life. I have
an eleven-acre field in which I grow corn, though young relatives do most of the work. We have two acres in the back
yard in which my wife and I keep a garden, much of it in
sweet corn and chile. My wife insists on growing onions,
carrots, cabbages, radishes, and tomatoes as well, like the
traditional Zuni woman she is. I do a lot of weeding. I also
work around the house, washing dishes, doing laundry,
cleaning, picking up the yard, feeding the dogs and the tur-
keys, and even cooking when she comes in tired from her
work in Gallup. She's a better cook than I am, though.

In the winter time I make silver and turquoise jewelry
when I have orders, usually from the Arabs who own the
tourist shops here in Zuni. I don't know how that came
about. We have had other white traders for so long that it
seemed natural. When I was a boy there were just a few
little grocery stores run by Whites with staples and clothes.
Zuni never had enough money to own stores then. A few
Zuni families would sell their pottery to the traders at ten
dollars a barrel for transport to urban markets back East,

but most business was done on credit, with accounts settled up when the lambs and wool were sold each spring. We didn't have pick-up trucks then to go to town and no money to buy anything if we had gone.

Today, we can drive to Gallup and get anything we want from the big stores there, but we can wholesale jewelry only to the Arabs here in Zuni. They export it to Europe and the Near East so they take in a large volume of merchandise. There is no other big market for us. Sometimes I take jewelry with me to Oklahoma when I go to visit my children and sell it at the big fiestas there at much better prices than the Arabs offer.

Although I can think in either Zuni or English, depending on what I'm doing, I have much less occasion to think in English now and regret it little. What I like best is to go to wherever I can find Zuni gathering, to the cafe or the post office, and talk to the people. It's the one thing I miss about public life. Otherwise, I am content with the life I lead, and have led, though I have missed much.

When I was young, I was told that I should pick the best from both cultures, the White man's and the Indian's, and make them part of my life. Thinking back to when I was a small boy, I can see that some things available to Whites are worth having. My indoor plumbing, central heating, electricity, television, clothes, and cars are all from the White world. I would not willingly do without them. Other, less material aspects of White culture, such as modern medicine and literacy, are even more important to me. On the other hand, if I never heard White music again, I would not miss it.

There are other things. It would not be right to grieve because I was never chosen to become a personator of the gods, but I know I have missed much. I have come to understand that the violent acts I have witnessed, and even done, make me unfit. A god personator must be able to hold nothing in his mind but the highest and holiest of thoughts. My mind was burned with too many wrong images.

I can still sit in judgment, making fair and thoughtful decisions to resolve disputes, as I have done many times as a council member. But having a judicial temperament is not the same as having a devout one. I can understand anger, how dangerous it is to one who harbors it and why disagreements must be resolved. Holy men must not deal with anger. People say I am successful as a judge when I sit with other members of the Council, but even being flexible is not an acceptable way for a religiously inclined person to act. There are right ways of doing things that were given to the Zuni by the gods, and we should follow them.

My Zuni friends say that I make too much of the distinction between the sacred and everyday worlds. Maybe it's because I've lived so much surrounded by white culture. The Zuni tend to see everything as sacred. When they see differences, it is between those things that can be approached without risk, such as water and corn, and those that need special preparation and care, like sacred masks. Water and corn are as sacred as masks, just not as dangerous to handle. A baby could play with them. Masks are dangerous because the spirit of a god resides in them and only persons who are trained and ritually pure can touch them safely.

And yet, I feel most a Zuni in the wintertime when the great Shalako festival is celebrated. I love everything about it. I particularly love the Shalako themselves, the giant birds

who are the messengers of the gods. There is something
about them, their ten-foot height and their irritability with
the clowning mudheads, that compels belief. I am a rational
man. I know that the Shalako is a dance-drama performed
by superbly trained god personators wearing sacred masks.
It doesn't lessen the beauty of it for me to know that. And
the old men who initiated me when I was a boy were right.
The gods do exist and are present in the dance.

The Zuni believe that in the beginning, it was the gods
themselves who came to visit the people in Zuni. The
people loved them so much that sometimes a Zuni man or
woman would follow them out of the village when they left.
Of course, that meant that the Zuni man or woman had to
die, for only the dead go to the dancehall under the sacred
lake. To spare the people from losing loved ones, the gods
stopped coming in person. They taught the people dances
and how to make masks so the relationship between the
gods and the people could continue. The Zuni believe that
the dances must be given every year if the Zuni world is to
survive. If the Zuni do not survive, what will happen to the
world outside of Zuni? We Zuni believe that the outside
world, too, would cease to exist.

I sometimes wonder what Whites or even Navajos think
about when they watch the Shalako dances. Can they feel
the presence of the gods? They certainly can't understand
what the songs the gods dance to are all about. Only a Zuni
can understand the words, and even Zuni must reflect on
them to get the deeper meaning. I have been doing that a lot
lately.

On the morning when the Shalako come to the village, I
can see them from my kitchen window before they enter

the pueblo. They walk single file, but they stop and talk among themselves from time to time. I wonder what it is gods find to talk about. Don't they know everything?

We tell our children that in the beginning there were just the five: Awonawilona, who is the living sky, the essence of life; Father Sun and Mother Moon above; and the divine pair, Shiwona and his wife, Shiwonokia, below. All was fog.

Awonawilona breathed from the heart, as only gods do, and blew the fog into clouds and into the waters of the earth. The god breathed from the heart and shared its essence with everything that was or will be. When Shiwona spat into his left hand and patted the spittle with his right, making rainbow bubbles which he blew into the air to form the stars, the stars took their essence from the breath of Awonawilona. When Shiwonokia spat into her hand, patted it into bubbles like the suds from yucca root, and let the suds overflow her hand, streaming everywhere to form the earth, it took its essence from the breath of Awonawilona.

Then Father Sun looked down and impregnated bits of foam with his rays, bringing forth two sons of his own. To each he gave a rainbow, lightning arrows, and a cloud shield, telling them to release the living things that dwelt in the underground. The divine children split the earth with their lightning arrows and went searching for living things. They found them crawling over each other in the dark, four levels down. Our emergence story tells of the adventures the people encountered on the way to the surface of the land, the journey which led the people into the light. Once on the surface, the people sought the center of the earth for their permanent abode. Zuni is built there. In fact, the ceremonial room of the Rain Priest of the North is built over the exact spot.

Some of the children were lost along the way, becoming the gods who went to live in the dancehall under the lake, Kothluwalawa. These are the gods who come to visit Zuni in spirit form during Shalako. That's how they started. The Zuni people are made from the same god-stuff. The gods are the lost children of our ancestors.

The old men tell us that the Shalako is a serious ceremonial for the whole world, not just for the Zuni. We live at the center of the earth and what we do affects the whole world, not just the Zuni. So many things can go wrong. The restrictions placed upon the personators are most strict and must be obeyed rigidly. The men must eat no meat, no fat, no salt, and no White men's food. Above all, there is a period when they are forbidden to speak with any women, even their mothers.

When the personators are in the kiva, the ceremonial house, or when they are costuming for the dance, they must not be observed. In the old days, Navajo were always coming around to watch. Now, it's tourists. If the performers are seen, or if they break any of the other restrictions, they may fall when they engage in the races that are part of the ceremonial. After dancing all night they are very tired, and if a rule has been broken or their hearts are not ritually pure, they may fall. This is a sign that the gods know the broken faith. The old men think on these matters and sometimes say that a disaster elsewhere in the world was caused by a Shalako falling. How they know is a mystery, one I do not question.

All of this makes more sense when I think it in Zuni. Sometimes I find it is impossible to explain things in English. For instance, some of my White friends collect what they call "Indian arrowheads." They classify them and date them and even duplicate them in their archeology laboratories. How can I tell them that the Zuni never made arrowheads? We found them on the ground, just like the White collectors do now. The Zuni believe that the arrowheads are the tips of lightning bolts thrown by the gods. We have no tradition of ever having made them, nor have I ever met another Pueblo Indian who claimed differently. In Zuni, the word for these items is not "Indian arrowhead," but "tip of a lightning bolt."

Sometimes I make fetishes for young Zuni runners who come to me because I once ran fast like they do now. I still run, but not fast. With sinew I attach arrowheads to the backs of fetishes, rocks carved to look like animals, and the runners wear them around their necks or tie them to their shoes so they will be swift as the lightning. Would they do that if they thought of the arrowheads as man-made? When I give them the fetishes they hold them in their hands close to their mouths and suck in their breath to inhale the sacred essence of Awonawilona that is in everything, even rocks, but particularly in the arrowheads. It is the Zuni way.

But the coming of the Shalako also has something of the feeling that the coming of Christmas has for White children. The difference is that, among the Zuni, the parents believe in the Shalako just as fervently as the children do. Imagine what it would be like if White adults believed in Santa Claus!

Those who are to personate the gods are chosen at the end of the festival that marks the beginning of the winter season. There are six Shalako personators chosen, with six alternates, along with others to personate the Council of the Gods, the weather gods, and the Koyemski, the sacred clowns that Whites call mudheads.

The ritual number for the Zuni is six. There are six cardinal directions: north, south, east, and west, along with up and down. There are also six kiva groups; membership is determined by the kiva group of the husband of the midwife who first touches the baby as he emerges from the womb. Someone in each kiva group is chosen to prepare his house to entertain one of the Shalako when they bring in the gods. Another house is chosen to entertain the Council of the Gods, and yet another to entertain the mudheads, eight houses in all.

No individual family is required to carry the expense by itself. All the men in the kiva group are expected to work on the Shalako houses, and the families of the members of the god cults work on the other two houses. The women prepare great quantities of food, not only to feed the participants and the Zuni people, but all of the many visitors who come. No one is turned away, not even the old arch enemy Navajo. The one exception used to be Hispanics, but that prejudice had historical roots. The Spanish first came to Zuni in 1540, hoping to find the fabled Seven Cities of Cibola glowing with gold. Instead, they found adobe houses and people whose idea of wealth was macaw feathers. The missionizing priests who accompanied the Spanish, and others who came after, viewed the Zuni ceremonies as diabolism. They did their best to stamp them out. The memories of the Zuni are long and the recollections bitter in the minds of the old men. The younger generation no longer thinks that way.

My earliest recollections are about the Shalako. I have a clear memory of being with my father in the very early morning watching the Shalako. They'd been up all night, dancing while I slept. They were enormous! They stood so tall as they rushed up and down the room, swooping and clacking their beaks at the mudheads, that I was frightened. I cried, but my father took me on his lap and told me not to cry, that they wouldn't hurt me. Snuggled in his arms, I wasn't afraid any more. I must have been three. My mother died soon after, and I was told she'd gone to Kothluwalawa to dance with the Shalako. I've loved them ever since.

They tell me that the Council of the Gods speaks to the one named "Owner of the Springs," who lives in Kothluwalawa, and they request permission to bring water to those Zuni who have performed rain dances and planted prayer plumes. With Owner of the Springs approval, couriers are sent to the rain gods, who live at the six corners of the earth, to bring rain to Zuni. Clouds appear and it rains, but the rain does not fall from the clouds in Zuni belief. The clouds mask the presence of the shadow folk, those who have died and live most of the time in Kothluwalawa, like my mother. It is the shadow folk who carry the pots and baskets of water to the Zuni, sprinkling it, or sometimes pouring it, through the clouds onto the earth. I have always known that I would rejoin my mother one day.

The Shalako never change for me. There is more than the constancy of the costume and the ritual of the dance itself. There is the walking at night to a Shalako house, when I can smell roasting chile and corn, fresh baked bread, smoke from pinon burning in the fireplaces. There is the snow that is always on the ground, and the cold air that makes everything smell better. There is the feeling of expectancy. Nowadays, the electric lights are jarring and the bumper-to-bumper traffic annoying and harder to ignore, but I can shut my mind to them.

It is hard for me to lose myself in the spectacle because of who I am. Now, when I come to a Shalako house, people move aside to let me enter and someone vacates a chair for me to sit down. I ignore the muttered protests of Whites who resent my stepping ahead of them, and pretend not to hear the whispered explanation, "That's Virgil!"

I sit and let the sound of the singing wash over me, concentrating on the words, watching the interplay between the Shalako and the mudheads, and I think back to the time I first saw them, with my father. I sometimes wish I had a child or a grandchild of my own to take into my lap and reassure on seeing his first Shalako. I no longer try to stay awake all night, but usually visit two or three houses for an hour before going back to my own home.

After the coming of electricity to Zuni, I used to worry about the continuity of the ceremonial itself. I remember coming back from the war and finding that I was an outsider, but that was not as bad as returning to Zuni from Gallup after electricity first came to the pueblo. When I was a teenager, I could sing katcina songs. The teenagers of the fifties sang songs by Chubby Checker, rock and roll songs they learned from the radio. They didn't even want to talk Zuni anymore, preferring some teenage kind of language based roughly on English.

I'd read Matilda Coxe Stevenson's accounts of Zuni when I was at the University of New Mexico after the war. She said that by 1896 the Shalako had already degenerated into a drunken brawl, with every male in Zuni (except the ceremony participants, of course) more interested in drinking than in the ceremonial. She would be surprised to see the Shalako of today. No one drinks now at Shalako.

Nearly every family in Zuni has a silversmith, and there is more money in the pueblo now than in the old days. Our young people have taken a new pride in their Indian heritage. There is even less drinking now, though it still remains a problem for some of the older Zuni, particularly the ex-G.I.'s. I lost my own brother, Lee, to drink. He never listened to me or to anyone else about how dangerous it was to drink and drive. He had a car wreck while drunk, and they pulled him out in a coma. He stayed that way for several years, dying at last in Meadows State Hospital in Las Vegas without ever recovering consciousness.

I never had any trouble with alcohol, but I came close once. Shortly after I got married the second time, my new wife noticed I'd developed the habit of taking a beer from the refrigerator as soon as I came home from work, then another, and another. She said, "Stop! I lost my first husband to alcoholism and I don't ever want to go through anything like that again." I stopped. It was close.

There are other kinds of problems now, perhaps brought on by too much easy money. Whereas private life has improved, public life has not. There are too many scandals about our tribal politicians, so many that people stop me in the street and ask me when I am going to run for governor and clean it all up. One man recently reminded me that I promised the old Sun Chief before he died that I would run for Governor after I retired. It's true. I did promise. Maybe I wasn't supposed to rest. Maybe there's a need for old "Honest Zuni" once again. Yes, I'll have to think about it.

HISTORICAL SKETCH
Carroll L. Riley

*T*oday, the Zuni tribe of western New Mexico is a flourishing part of modern America, helping to give a multicultural flavor and richness to our country. The history of Zuni Pueblo is one strand of a great Native American web of histories, stretching back to the Ice Age. Understanding the past of the Zuni people enriches our perception of their future. Virgil Wyaco and his story are a microcosm of that past and future, and to comprehend the details of Virgil's own life it is necessary to know something of the pueblo of his origin.

At the heart of modern Zuni, a group of venerable flat-roofed houses cluster around a restored mission church that dates from the seventeenth century. The modern gas stations and shops along the main thoroughfare are interspersed with dwellings of native stone, built many decades ago. The tidy suburban homes on the outer perimeters of the town could be part of any small semi-rural community in North America. Farming outliers stretch from Ojo Caliente in the southwest to Nutria some twenty-five miles to the northeast, and the northwest horizon is broken by a pair of severe mesas, the Zuni Twin Buttes. Overshadowing it all is Dowa Yalanne, Zuni's sacred mountain, a mesa lying about three miles southeast of town. A massive headland of rusty red and creamy white sandstones, it rises majestically several hundred feet above the riverine plain. At the time of European contact, in the sixteenth century, lands used—at least sporadically—by the Zuni extended westward to San Francisco Peak in Arizona, northward to Steamboat Wash, eastward to Mt. Taylor, and southward to the Salt and Gila Basins. In later times, the U.S. government compressed this territory into a reservation covering a mere 636 square miles, bordered by the state of Arizona and extending along the upper valley of the Zuni River.

Central to Zuni life is the Zuni River. A small stream rising in high country near the Continental Divide, it drains westward from the western slopes of the Zuni Mountains. At Black Rock, about five miles east of the modern pueblo, the river flows into the Zuni Basin, a broad alluvial valley that extends southwestward. The river meanders through the valley, eventually joining the upper Little Colorado River near the town of St. Johns in what is now northeastern Arizona. Though the Zuni River is intermittent in its lower course, forming a series of waterholes, it usually flows throughout the year in the upper reaches, fed by springs in the Ramah and Pescado areas and by Nutria Creek. This is all relatively high country. The altitude at modern Zuni Pueblo is a little over 6,400 feet, with the mesa country to the south reaching elevations of 7,000 feet or more. The highest point on Dowa Yalanne is about 7,100 feet.

At the beginning of historic times, the Zuni utilized virtually all of their country. They hunted and gathered wild plants in the Zuni Mountains and farmed along the river. A major ceremonial center at Kothluwalawa, a shallow lake near the junction of the Zuni and the Little Colorado, has had religious significance to the Zuni people from prehistoric times to the present.

The vegetation of the Zuni area has not changed signifi- cantly for the past several hundred years, and today, as in the past, it varies considerably with altitude. In the upper reaches of the Zuni Mountains larger conifers grow, as do various oaks. Along the slopes of the mesas above the Zuni River are groves of piñon and juniper as well as saltbush, sagebrush, and various cacti, and gambel, Arizona white, and emory oak. The river bottoms have juniper, oak, cottonwood, rabbit brush, sage, and cholla. Precipitation levels also vary with altitude, with more moisture in the higher elevations. Zuni Pueblo gets about twelve inches of precipitation per year, which falls mostly as rain during the summer months, making dry farming possible at Zuni. The growing season is rather short as there are occasional frosts as late as the end of May and as early as mid-September.

Animal life in the past has included large carnivores such as mountain lion, bobcat, bear, and wolf. These animals, like the human beings of the region, have hunted a variety of browsers and vegetation eaters including deer, pronghorn, mountain sheep, rabbits and jackrabbits, chipmunks, and ground squirrels. Bison probably did not extend this far west, but the Zuni did obtain bison products through trade. The region has always supported numbers of birds: various songbirds, water birds, and such raptors as the hawk and eagle. All Pueblo Indians put ceremonial importance on birds, using the feathers in a variety of rites and ceremonies. Historically, these have included not only locally available birds but also ones traded up from Mexico, especially the bright-plumaged macaws and parrots.

There are a few edible fish in the Zuni and upper Little Colorado Rivers. However, the Zuni, like their Little Colorado neighbors the Hopi, have never been fish eaters, actually having fish taboos that relate to the Zuni origin stories. Reptiles such as rattlesnakes and turtles, as well as amphibian toads and frogs, also figure in the origin tales. There is the normal insect and arachnid population, and, as might be expected, bats are also common.

The following sketch of Zuni origins is one derived from modern archaeology and history. It tells a different story from the traditional religious accounts of the Zuni people. This does not mean that one version is "correct" and the other "false," simply that the Zuni approach history with a different mind-set and world view. To better understand this, suppose we turn things around! If a Zuni historian, not raised in the Christian tradition, were to study the life and times of Jesus, he would first find a folk philosopher wandering over the highways and byways of Galilee, teaching his little cluster of disciples a commonsense doctrine of individual responsibility and moral worth. This teacher then disappears, and it is not entirely clear from present evidence what happened to him. Next, our Zuni historian would find another doctrine, which appeared twenty years later, linking a man—also called Jesus—to an ancient and widespread fertility ritual of a god who died and was resurrected. A centuries-old Jewish legend of a messiah is added in, and Jesus becomes a mythical figure, the "Christ." The Zuni scholar would surely classify the teachings about this mythological second individual as a rather primitive superstition. But to the practicing Christian, Jesus of Galilee and the Risen Christ are undivided parts of an divine revelation that is the central event of human affairs, the hinge of history.

The point is that modern Anglo-American anthropologists and historians (whether believers or not) are part of the Judeo-Christian tradition. Such people must understand that their reconstruction of Zuni culture, like our Zuni historian's reconstruction of Christianity, does not account for the transcendental interpretations of human affairs. Both the great Zuni deity Awonawilona and Jesus Christ have their separate species of "reality."

Until around nine thousand years ago the northern parts of the earth were covered by massive glaciations, the last phase of a long geologic period called the Pleistocene or Ice Age. During the terminal Ice Age, we know that human beings, Paleoindians of the Clovis tradition, lived in what is now New Mexico, having first entered the region over eleven thousand years ago. Clovis and later big game hunters such as Folsom were concentrated farther to the east in the Rio Grande region and the high plains. Still, occasional hunting or foraging parties did reach the Zuni, for Paleoindian spear points are found on mesas in the Zuni area.

As time went on, the glaciers disappeared from the North American continent, and Southwestern climates became considerably drier, with hot summers and mild winters. Possibly as early as 6,500 B.C. little groups of gatherers and hunters, the Archaic peoples, who had developed methods of living in harsh desert environments, began to infiltrate the area from the west. By around 2,000 B.C. the Zuni area was becoming a border region between two major Archaic traditions, the Oshara to the east and the Cochise to the west and south.

Beginning some time before 1,000 B.C. a dramatic change took place in the Archaic cultures of the Southwest. Ideas about the planting and harvesting of certain food plants, originally developed in what is now southern and eastern Mexico, began to spread throughout the region. These plants—maize, cotton, and squash, then a few centuries later, beans—gradually made their way into the Southwest, enriching and changing the old conservative Archaic cultures. By the early centuries of the Christian, or Common, era three major cultures were appearing in the Southwest. One was the Hohokam of the middle Gila River, and a second was the Mogollon of the upper Gila and Salt River drainages. Both of these were descendants of the Cochise. The third, the Anasazi from an Oshara base, lived farther east and north. The Hohokam had relatively little influence on the prehistoric Zuni, but the Mogollon and Anasazi were the bases from which came the Zuni people.

The early agricultural Mogollon and Anasazi peoples lived at first in villages of unconnected pit houses, structures whose floors were excavated several inches to several feet below the surface. The excavated pit-house walls formed an integral part of the house walls, which were usually made of interwoven poles smeared with mud. Roofs were sometimes supported by upright posts or sometimes rested directly on the house walls. One significant invention, that of pottery, may have appeared first to people who were ancestral both to Hohokam and Mogollon. These peoples made a plainware pottery, which among the Mogollon developed into a series of brown or red wares. About A.D. 400, the idea of pottery spread northward to the Anasazi, and within a century or so the Anasazi peoples began to produce their own distinctive gray-white pottery. Over the next five or six hundred years a vigorous Anasazi tradition with large towns and irrigation agriculture developed in the Chaco

Canyon and other parts of the San Juan River system in New
Mexico. At the same time large pueblos of Mogollon type
were growing up in the mountain reaches of the Gila drainage. West-central New Mexico was, therefore, an early
meeting ground of the Mogollon and Anasazi ceramic traditions. What is later called "Western Pueblo," ancestral
Zuni and Hopi, is an amalgam of Mogollon and Anasazi
traits, and the historic Zuni benefit from this rich dual
heritage.

One curious thing about the Zuni is their language. Recent studies suggest that the Zuni tongue is only distantly related to the other Pueblo languages—Shoshonean Hopi to
the northwest, and Keresan and Tanoan to the east—and
not at all to the nearby Apache and Navajo languages. From
what direction the Zuni language came to reach the Zuni region is not known with any certainty but it may have been
from the Mogollon region to the west and south. By the sixteenth century, as far as we know, Zuni was restricted to the
Cíbolan towns, though it should be remembered that the
evidence is anything but complete.

In the early 1300s at least fifteen very large stone and
mud masonry towns were scattered through the upper and
middle Zuni River valley. One of these sites, called Halonawa, was on or near the present Zuni Pueblo but south of
Zuni River. This and several other sites were deserted by
the latter part of the fourteenth century. A new Halonawa
(called Halonawa North by archaeologists) was built about
A.D. 1400 north of the Zuni River.

At roughly that time the Zuni area included ten major
towns. These were spread out from southwest to northeast
in the Zuni River drainage. Most southwesterly were the
towns of Kechibawa and Hawikuh, and a few miles to the

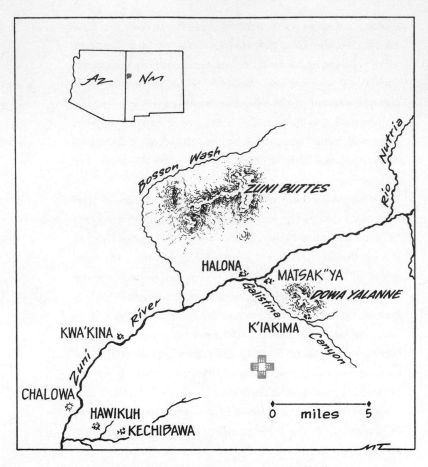

Zuni Area in the Mid-Sixteenth Century. Map by Michael Taylor.

northwest of Hawikuh was Chalowa on the north side of the Zuni River. Farther east, also on the north bank of the river, was the somewhat smaller pueblo of Kwa'kina. Eastward and on the south side of the river were Hambassawa and Binnawa, likewise rather small. Halonawa North or, to use its shortened form, Halona, was at the site of the present Zuni Pueblo, while Matsak'ya was in the river flats south

of the Zuni River a few miles east of the modern city center. K'iakima, farther south, lay on the south-facing slope
of Dowa Yalanne. A tenth, recently discovered, late prehistoric town was Ahkyaya, situated on the north side of the
river, near modern Black Rock.

The rock-and-mud-mortar Zuni pueblos of this "protohistoric" period were made of contiguous rooms grouped
around plazas and sometimes reaching several stories. The
ruins are rich in bichrome and polychrome painted pottery.
Beginning around A.D. 1300 there had appeared a new type
of pottery decoration achieved by adding designs on the pot
faces with paints that contained lead ores. When the pots
were fired these paints spread as glazing over portions of the
vessels. The Zuni area was probably an important progeni-
tor of the glaze wares that became so important in the Rio
Grande basins from the fourteenth century on into Spanish
times.

Another defining feature of the area, cremation of the
dead, had spread to the Zuni pueblos after A.D. 1400, certainly from the south and west. It was never universally
adopted, but in the westernmost Zuni pueblos about a third
of all burials in the protohistoric period were cremations
(there are no reliable data for the eastern Zuni towns). The
custom spread eastward into the Rio Grande Valley and as
far east as the Tompiro pueblos in the Estancia Valley east of
the Manzano Mountains. It was practiced sporadically, however, and the cremations that took place in these areas may
simply represent instances of specific Zuni influence, exer-
cised perhaps by trading parties.

Probably the most important feature of the protohistoric
Zuni pueblos is that in the early fifteenth century they became centers and trans-shipment points for trade. Major

trading trails ran south into northeastern Sonora, where good-sized towns along sections of the major rivers were organized into what are sometimes called "statelets." This trade involved shell, copper, brightly plumaged macaws and parrots, and perhaps cotton cloth. The Zuni trans-shipped these goods eastward to exchange for bison skins, pottery, and the beautiful schist, fibrolite from Pecos Pueblo. Even more important was turquoise from mines in the Rio Grande Valley. The Zuni region produced salt and certain semi-precious stones, garnet and peridots, which also went along the trails to the south. At the same time, the Zuni traded with Hopi, receiving dyed and woven cotton and pottery. In cooperation with the Hopi, traders from Zuni were able to tap the shell and coral sources in the Gulf of California and the Pacific Coast.

The trade opened up Zuni to new products and new ideas. One enormously important happening was the introduction of the *kachina* cult out of Mexico some time after A.D. 1300. It now looks as if this important religious cult spread out of the old Casas Grandes area of Chihuahua and diffused up the Rio Grande to the Eastern Pueblos and along the trade routes westward to Zuni and Hopi. The religious centrality of the kachinas (or *koko* as they are called at Zuni) to the Pueblo world in late prehistoric times can hardly be doubted. The cult featured masked figures that represented ancestors. These masked dancers still visit Zuni at certain times of the year and perform colorful and religiously satisfying rituals. They bring fertility, rain, good will, and prosperity to the Zuni and to all peoples. They live under the sacred lake, Kothluwalawa, where, after death, the Zuni individual confidently expects to join them.

The kachina cult, though it has a very Southwestern fla-

vor, still shows strong signs of its origin in Mesoamerica.
It seems basically to be a cult of Tlaloc, the rain deity of ancient Mexico, but it also has strong affinities with Quetzalcoatl, whose name means both sacred twin and plumed
serpent, and who also represents the planet Venus as morning and evening star. Both Tlaloc and the great god Quetzalcoatl are venerable, their origins lost in the mists of antique
times.

Among modern Pueblos, the kachina cult is much diluted
in the east because of the seventeenth-century attempt by
Franciscan missionaries to eradicate it. The Franciscans considered the masked dances to be diabolic in nature and
fought the cult tooth and nail. They did not succeed entirely, and the Pueblo Revolt of 1680 was in part a reaction
to this repression of the kachinas. Still, some damage was
done, and today only in Zuni and Hopi can kachinas be seen
in their full glory.

Only general statements can be made about the Zuni so-
ciopolitical and religious systems of late pre-Hispanic times.
From the reports of the Coronado party in 1540, there is
reason to believe that, at least for religious purposes, the
then six Zuni towns had some sort of cooperative arrangement in their ceremonialism. Possibly, they took turns at
hosting the various summer and winter ceremonies. There
may also have been a loose coordination of political functions. This, in turn, would have been enhanced by the
kachina cult, whose members and functions were present in
each of the towns.

The cult appeared among the Pueblos at a time of great
crisis. The San Juan region with its great towns of Chaco
and the Mesa Verde region had collapsed, and there was extensive migration. Perhaps 30,000 people relocated from

the San Juan Basin to the Rio Grande to the east, or to the Western Pueblo region (including Zuni) to the west. The mechanisms for regional governance in the Chaco region, whatever form they took, were then lost, and the new kachina cult crosscut the older kin-based structures, creating new avenues for interpersonal cooperation. The cult may well have served to knit the rapidly growing towns, and also to provide a mechanism for intertown cooperation. In the Zuni towns, at least in historic times, all male members of a pueblo were expected to be members of the cult, achieving membership through the six kiva groups. The kiva groups, by the way, had color-directional symbolism. This suggests considerable antiquity, for such symbolism is widespread not only in Mesoamerica but in continental North America.

Zuni religion, at the coming of the Spaniards, clearly emphasized the supreme life-giving force that was called Awonawilona. Under Awonawilona were other supernatural figures. Some may have gone back thousands of years in the Southwest, while others like Kolowisi, the plumed serpent, and the twin war gods (manifestations of Quetzalcoatl and the morning and evening star) were widespread in Mesoamerica and probably represented adaptations during Pueblo times, even if certain of them date from several centuries before the Spaniards came.

The twin war gods had their earthly epiphany in the Older and Younger Bow Priests of the bow priesthood. There is some reason to believe that in the early fourteenth century, contemporary with the kachina cult, organizations like the bow priesthood, relating to war and trading, appeared among the Pueblos. In late prehistoric times this bow priesthood probably had a military and police function as it does today. It also seems likely that, because of its quasi-military function, some trading activities were in the hands of the bow priesthood.

Certain of the curing and hunting societies also seem to have developed during these disturbed but active and innovative times. Like the kachina cult these various polities crosscut kin groups and led to wider cooperation within and among towns. There were also the rain priesthoods, whose members, at least today, are generally chosen through matrilineal descent. Rain priests have the production of rain as an overriding function. Their ceremonials are conducted in various households that contain sacred objects or *fetishes*. Their rites, today, are basically private, as they may have been in late prehistoric times.

Zuni, on the eve of Spanish intervention, probably had a number of curing and hunting societies associated with beast gods, especially predator animals who were, and continue to be, considered to have strong curing powers. Today, there are twelve of these societies, with both men and women holding membership. An exception is the male-only *sutikanne* hunting society. Masks and other ceremonial objects were and are believed to have great power at Zuni and among Pueblos generally. In the hands of people ritually unprepared to handle these objects, they are considered very dangerous. Even copies of such sacred objects may be dangerous. For example, there are today ten *koyemshi* (sometimes called "mud heads") or ceremonial clowns, and each of their costumes is one of a kind, filled with power and never to be replicated. The American scholar, Frank Cushing, is known to have copied a koyemshi mask and actually demonstrated it for a Smithsonian photographer. Cushing's illness and early death are thought by the Zuni to be the result of his wanton and reckless misuse of this sacred gear.

Interlocking firmly with the religious groups are the basic

social units of Zuni. Today there are fifteen Zuni clans. The exact count as of late pre-Hispanic times is unknown but it was probably about the same. The clans gradually changed over time as some became too small to be viable, while other large ones developed subclans, which eventually broke off and formed clans in their own right. This process continues today. Clans are matrilineal, that is descended through the female line, and houses and household goods are owned by women. Men live in their wives' houses on sufferance as it were. In the event of the breakup of a family, the man will move back to the home of his mother or sister, which individuals belonged to the same primary clan. The father's clan is not without importance, however, and its significance is perhaps most evident in certain ceremonial situations.

In pre-Hispanic days the bow priesthood was in charge of secular functions, but today Spanish-introduced officers, including the council members and governor, control many of the secular functions. Nevertheless, priestly influence over all aspects of society was very strong indeed, and even today it would be somewhat misleading to speak of a secular/religious division of Zuni life.

The trade network discussed above undoubtedly enriched the lives of Southwesterners, including the Zuni, but it also led to one unfortunate consequence. Trade trails were of course two-way passages, and beginning probably in the early 1530s the Zuni and other Southwesterners heard vague rumors of dramatic events as a new people invaded western Mexico. Spanish interest in the Southwest began with the story told to Nuño Beltrán de Guzmán, a bloodthirsty conquistador, who in the period 1529–32 plundered and murdered his way from Jalisco to Sinaloa, devastating and largely depopulating the western Mexican coast. In the year 1530 Guzmán had been informed by an Indian servant from east-central Mexico of a rich land to the north, where seven great cities existed and where people were rich in precious metals. The theme of seven cities was European— the Seven Cities of Antillia, settled by seven Portuguese bishops, who with their congregations fled the Moors in the eighth century.

Searching for the "seven cities," Guzmán penetrated western coastal Mexico as far as central Sinaloa, where he founded a city, Culiacán, a few miles south of the modern west Mexican metropolis. Guzmán was soon called home by a Spanish government unhappy with his excesses, but his settlers at Culiacán continued to raid northward, seeking slaves. In 1533, Diego de Guzmán, a kinsman of the conqueror, led one such slave raid as far at the lower Yaqui River. A push on northward would have been inevitable in any case, but it was hurried along in the summer of 1536 by the arrival in Culiacán of a group of four wanderers. These men, three Spanish soldiers and a black slave, had been shipwrecked several years earlier on the east Texas coast and had been slowly working their way west. They succeeded in part because of the leadership skills of their commander, Alvar Nuñez Cabeza de Vaca, and because of the language-learning and other survival abilities of the slave, Esteban de Dorantes.

Near the end of their journey, Cabeza de Vaca and his party had been entertained by peoples in the statelet area of northeast Sonora. There they heard of great towns to the north with massive "apartment-like" buildings and inhabitants who were eager for the trade in shell and brightly colored feathers. In return, the northerners shipped precious turquoise and other goods to the statelet towns. The Sonoran people were describing the Zuni towns, which they knew first-hand from visits of their own traders to Zuni and second-hand from descriptions by Zuni individuals visiting or living in the statelet area.

About the time the Cabeza de Vaca party reached Mexico, news was flooding in of the Spanish conquest of the gold-rich Inca Empire. Gold seemed to be everywhere, and the viceroy in Mexico City, Antonio Mendoza, quickly organized a large expedition to the Southwest. He was egged on by the fact that one of the Inca conquerors, Hernando De Soto, was in the process of launching a huge expedition through Florida into the interior of North America. In order to forestall De Soto, Viceroy Mendoza sent his own exploratory expedition in the spring of 1539. For its leader he chose a Franciscan friar, Marcos de Niza, formerly with Pizarro in Peru. Aiding and guiding Marcos was Esteban, the black slave from the Cabeza de Vaca party. With these two went a number of Indians, some from central or west Mexico but various of them Piman-speaking natives who had come south with Cabeza de Vaca three years previously.

Staying near the coast, the small Marcos expedition worked its way through Sinaloa and Sonora, eventually reaching the town of Vacapa, probably in the Piman-speaking area of the Magdalena or Altar Valleys. Esteban de Dorantes pushed on north with part of the Indian contingent to spy out the land. Four days later, messengers dispatched by Esteban came back to Vacapa, one of them a native of the region north of Vacapa, who told of a kingdom or province of seven large cities called Cíbola. With this mention, the Zuni people enter world history.

Cíbola is probably a corruption of the word *shiwana* the

Zuni name for their homeland. However, Edmund Ladd, who is both an anthropologist and a Zuni, has suggested that Cíbola might be a misunderstanding of the Zuni term for bison, *si:wolo*. Certainly, bison hides were one of the trade items moving out of Cíbola to the north and west Mexican area, reshipped from sources farther to the east. In any case, Marcos had news of Zuni. Following behind Esteban, he reached the outskirts of the Zuni pueblos in the late spring of 1539, where he heard the dreadful news that Esteban had been killed outside one of the Cíbolan towns. Some of the Indians with Esteban had been captured, but others had fled to give Marcos the news.

According to his own account Marcos pushed on north, having bribed his frightened Indian followers to accompany him. Some time around the middle of May in the Julian calendar he reached one of the "seven cities," either Hawikuh or the more easterly town of K'iakima on the south flank of Dowa Yalanne. Viewing the settlement at sunset across a broad valley, Marcos decided that it was larger than the city of Mexico, and he retreated to the south. Aside from his exaggerated perception of the size of his Zuni town, there was one serious error in his account, Marcos somehow having the idea that Cíbola lay near the Gulf of California. This misapplication of geography was then incorporated into the logistic planning for the Spanish expedition launched the next year. It was to have dire consequences for the Spaniards.

Francisco Vázquez de Coronado, who led the expedition of 1540 to the Southwest, interviewed Zuni Indians the year after Esteban's death. He reported that the Zuni had been influenced by stories from the Chichilticalli region of southeastern Arizona about Esteban causing the death of women there. As Esteban and his party were moving very rapidly northward, it seems unlikely that any such stories could have reached the Zuni before Esteban appeared. According to Coronado, Esteban also assaulted Zuni women. Esteban does seem to have been somewhat of a Don Juan, but it is doubtful that he had any sort of relationship with the women of Zuni.

Much more likely is the possibility that the Zuni feared Esteban both as a witch and as a spy for the sinister pale-skinned groups who were ravaging the country to the south. Where the black slave was killed is not certain. Later stories of the "chili-lipped black man" that were told to Cushing in the 1880s indicate that he died at K'iakima. If this is true, it lends some credence to the idea that Marcos may also have seen K'iakima rather than Hawikuh.

Following Marcos' report, Viceroy Mendoza appointed his young protégé Vázquez de Coronado to lead an expedition northward. The army was enormous by contemporary standards. There were some 350 Spanish soldiers, perhaps 1,200 armed Indian allies drawn from central Mexico and from the Tarascan region, plus an unknown number of Indian and black slaves and servants. There were horses and mules, sheep, perhaps some cattle—a livestock total of 1,500 or more. An additional naval contingent with three ships under the command of Hernando de Alarçón carried part of the supplies.

This unwieldy army moved on to Culiacán, reaching that outpost around Easter time. There, Coronado decided to leave the slow-moving main army and advance with a vanguard of some seventy horsemen and twenty to thirty Spanish foot soldiers plus some of the Indian allies, a total of perhaps 200 to 300 individuals. It was this vanguard that first encountered the Zuni.

Coronado followed the well-known traders' trails that
snaked northward out of west Mexico to the land of the
Sonoran statelets. He then followed the Sonora River northward, eventually reaching the San Pedro in southern Arizona. The party traveled up that river to the Gila and finally
its tributary, the San Francisco River, in what is now western New Mexico. From the San Francisco the vanguard
eventually reached the upper drainage of the Carrizo Wash.
Coronado pushed westward along the Carrizo, briefly crossing again into modern Arizona. About eight miles from
where the Carrizo joins the Little Colorado it comes within
about three miles of the Zuni River. Coronado and his men
crossed this narrow neck of land into the Zuni drainage.
By this time the Spaniards, who were undersupplied, had
reached starvation point. Gold and treasures now became
less important than corn.

Coronado reached the Zuni area in the first week of July
by the Julian calendar, which corrected to Gregorian reckoning would be some time around mid-July. The summer
solstice had passed and the Zuni towns were surely involved
in their round of summer ceremonials. As mentioned earlier, there is some reason to believe that in the sixteenth
century there were reciprocal ceremonies held by all the
Zuni in one or another of the pueblos. The movement of
Zuni parties during these July days, suggests a ceremony
centered at Hawikuh, the largest western Pueblo. This particular ceremony seems to have involved a journey to the sacred Lake Kothluwalawa near the mouth of the Zuni River.
It is hard to overstate the lake's religious and emotional importance to the Zuni people, past and present, for it is the
entrance to the Zuni afterlife and the residence of the kachinas. Edmund Ladd believes that Coronado and his men

moved into the Zuni River area just as an important ceremony was going on. The columns of smoke in the Hawikuh
area that were reported by Coronado suggest ceremonial
activity.

After a skirmish somewhere on the Zuni River, west of
Hawikuh, Coronado attacked the town itself. The Hawikuh
warriors sent their women and children to the eastern Zuni
towns and made a good fight of it. In the flats outside of Hawikuh they rained arrows on the Spaniards, killing three of
the horses and wounding seven or eight others. The Zuni
then retired into the fortress-like pueblo and managed to
hold out for a time. They hurled heavy rocks including
metates down on the Spaniards and succeeded in knocking
Coronado off a ladder, rendering him unconscious for a
time. Several Spanish soldiers also received wounds, but
eventually superior firepower and the armor of the Spaniards forced the surrender of Hawikuh, or, as the Spaniards
renamed it, Granada. The great battle between the Zuni and
the Europeans was over.

Coronado and his soldiers do not seem to have abused the
Zuni, though they did loot the corn supplies. Of course we
have only the Spaniards' words for this, but from all the
evidence at hand it would seem that Coronado was generally conciliatory. In any case most of the Zuni had fled first
to other pueblos and eventually to the heights of Dowa
Yalanne. Over the next few months the Spaniards tried to
regularize their relationships with the Zuni, and expeditions were sent to Hopi and to the Colorado River. A trading party from Pecos Pueblo and the Rio Grande town of
Tiguex reached Zuni, and a Spanish party traveled back with
that party, eventually reaching the edge of the Plains.

Meanwhile, the main army, following the vanguard, finally reached Zuni some time in late November 1540. Coronado was becoming worried over the prospects of spending a winter in the Southwest. By now he was fully aware that the Gulf of California lay some hundreds of miles over mountain and desert to the southwest. Captain Hernando de Alarçón, leading the sea arm of the expedition, had reached the lower Colorado River but then was forced to turn back to west Mexico with his precious cargo of clothing and food for the army.

By November 1540, Coronado had decided to shift his entire army to the Rio Grande Valley. He was encouraged in this by the Zuni, who no doubt painted grim pictures of the winter climate at Zuni and the suffering that the underclad and undersupplied Spanish army would face. The Zuni also seem to have provided guides for a special party led by Coronado that marched across the southern flank of the Zuni Mountains, across the San Agustín Plain, to reach Piro country on the Rio Grande somewhere around modern Socorro.

With how many Zuni towns did Coronado actually have to deal? By the time the Spaniards arrived, the ten pueblos that had existed from the early fifteenth century had shrunk to six or possibly seven. Coronado and his men talked of seven cities, but they named only three towns. Marcos de Niza in 1539 contributed the name Cíbola, which he believed was a city as well as the name of the kingdom. Another city, which Marcos believed to be the principal city of the kingdom of Cíbola, was named Ahacus. This could conceivably have been Hawikuh. The chronicler of the Coronado expedition, Pedro de Castañeda, mentioned Mazaque (Matsak'ya). It is clear that Hambassawa, Binnawa, and Ahkyaya were deserted by the earliest Spanish times. It has been suggested that the large western pueblo of Chalowa could still have been occupied or have been deserted recently enough that it entered the count of seven. At any rate, by the early 1580s only six towns are known: Kechibawa, Hawikuh, Halona, Kwa'kina, Matsak'ya, and K'iakima.

The year 1541 saw relatively little activity at the various Zuni pueblos. Problems with the Sonoran outpost of San Gerónimo led to small Spanish parties traveling back and forth from that outpost to the main army in the Rio Grande Valley in 1541 and 1542. These almost certainly went through or by way of Zuni but we do not know what sort of interaction (if any) was involved.

The Spanish attempt to find gold in the Southwest proved a failure. Coronado, injured in a fall from his horse around the end of 1541, decided to return to Mexico. The numerous slaves taken in the sack of Tiguex (a group of Pueblos on the Rio Grande north of the Piro) a year earlier were ordered released, and the Spaniards turned westward from their headquarters on the Rio Grande. They reached Zuni probably in April 1542 and regrouped briefly there. Then the army turned southward, and for two or three days the Zuni people followed them, picking up discarded pieces of baggage and, at least according to the chronicler Castañeda, coaxing various of the Mexican Indian allies to stay behind.

Coaxed or not, a number of Coronado's auxiliary Mexicans did stay at Zuni and elsewhere. We are not sure of the numbers of these remaining Indians but 100 would not seem an excessive number and perhaps there were even more. From the expeditions of the early 1580s, we have the names of four of the resettlers, all living at Zuni. Two of these men were from the Mexico City area, the third from Tonalá, and the fourth from around Guadalajara. Two were probably Nahuatl- or Aztec-speaking, the other two probably Tarascan-speaking. Another unnamed man was mentioned for Pecos Pueblo. Against this very low head count we have the statement of Castañeda that quite a number of Mexican Indians stayed behind, especially at Zuni. It is likely that the few Mexican Indians who recontacted the Spaniards forty years after Coronado were not typical of the group as a whole. Indians deserting the Spanish cause in the far north of New Spain were probably disaffected individuals and presumably would have been no more eager to see Spaniards in 1582 than they had been in 1542.

In the forty-year interregnum, the people of Zuni, like all the Pueblo Indians, were free. In spite of the infusion of new blood from central Mexico, Zuni life had been left relatively unchanged by the first Spanish incursion. There is no real evidence that any of the uses of Christianity took hold at Zuni. The explorer Espejo mentioned seeing crosses in Zuni country in 1583. If in fact not star symbols, these may have been magical in nature. Even though the Spaniards left a flock of sheep, it did not survive the four decades between Coronado and the next Spanish parties. As far as is known, no other stock animals were left behind. The popular belief that the Southwest and Great Plains were stocked by stray horses left from the Coronado expedition is simply a myth, and horses did not become available to the Southwestern Indian population for a century or more. Nor was either Spanish or Mexican-Indian pottery introduced to the Zuni area. It would seem that there was no potter among the remainees. A certain amount of scrap iron was left behind, but it is unlikely that any of the Aztec or Tarascan deserters were skilled in iron work at this early date. In any case, no "Iron Age" developed in the Southwest as a result of the Coronado trip.

A few things do seem to date from this period, however.

There is some reason to think that watermelons and canta-
loupes managed to take hold in the Rio Grande from seed
brought by Coronado. We know that such melons were being grown in the Sonora Valley twenty years after Coronado
passed through, and melons found by the Oñate settlers in
the Rio Grande in 1598 were considered "native" as of that
period. Another innovation, a game called in the Southwest
patol—a form of the popular and widespread Mexican game
of *patolli*—may have reached the Pueblo area at this time. It
was certainly played at Zuni in historic times and the later
distribution of the game in the Southwest suggests a six-
teenth-century introduction.

The most intriguing possibility for evidence of Mexican
influence on the Southwest, specifically at Zuni and Hopi, is
the performance of the great year-end ritual, the *Shalako*.
Although some elements of the Shalako iconography are
clearly prehistoric, the Zuni Shalako has many tantalizing
similarities to a specific Aztec ceremonial called the *Teotleco*,
and it is tempting to believe that at least certain aspects of
this great ceremony were introduced by Indians remaining
at Zuni after Coronado.

We do know what was happening demographically at
Zuni during this middle part of the sixteenth century. At the
time of Coronado, as has been shown, there were six, or
just possibly seven, towns. The total population has been
variously estimated from 2,000 to 4,000 people. Perhaps
3,000 or even 3,500 would be a reasonable figure.

In the early 1580s two expeditions reached Zuni, that of
Chamuscado in late 1581 and the more wide-ranging expedition of Espejo in 1583. Members of these expeditions reported the six towns mentioned above. The Zuni were not
particularly disturbed by these expeditions as both were

small and, operating under the new laws of 1571, they were
circumscribed in their interaction with any of the native peoples. The Espejo expedition did get into a brief battle with Querechos, which led to the first mention of these Apachean peoples west of the Rio Grande. By 1580 the Querechos were roving as far as Hopi country and seemed to have a population center in the Acoma region. There is no specific mention of them around Zuni but the Zuni people were likely already in contact with these ancestors of the Navajo and Western Apache.

It was with the Chamuscado and Espejo expeditions that the word "Zuni" entered the Spanish lexicon. Both of these expeditions had gone by the Keresan-speaking pueblo of Acoma, and the Acoma word for the Cíbola people was pronounced something like "suni," which was sometimes written "Suni" or "Zuni," and sometimes "Zuñi." The latter is pronounced "zunyi"—the tilde over the n giving it an "ny" sound. This spelling was picked up by Oñate and became common usage, even though it is not a very accurate rendition of the Acoma word. Modern Zuni people prefer "Zuni" to "Zuñi."

Expeditions that reached the Rio Grande in 1590–91 and again in the period around 1594–95 do not seem to have influenced the Zuni at all. No doubt these visitors were monitored by cautious and worried Zuni bow priests because the excesses of Coronado could hardly have been forgotten. In 1590 Zuni still had a flourishing trade with the Eastern Pueblos as well as with Hopi and people in Sonora, but times were changing and changing very fast.

In the year 1598 the Spaniards came to stay. Juan de Oñate arrived with a colonizing party in the summer of that year. From his headquarters at San Juan de los Caballeros (the Tewa Pueblo of Okeh near the junction of the Rio Grande and Chama River) Oñate's settlers and missionaries quickly spread out across the Southwest. The Spaniards reached Zuni (probably Halonawa North) on November 1, 1598, and two days later marched on to Hawikuh, which they referred to as Cíbola, mentioning also that Coronado had renamed it Granada. At this time Zuni still had six pueblos, which Oñate listed in the "Act of Obedience and Vassalage" attested by two individuals, Negua Homi and Atiz Oha, who said that they were the chiefs of the six Zuni towns. One wonders exactly who these "chiefs" were and what they thought they were signing. The six pueblos were named as Aguicobe (Hawikuh), Canabi (Kechibawa), Coaquina (Kwa'kina), Holonagu (Halona), Mazaqui (Matsak'ya), and Aquima (K'iakima). The signing suggests that there was some sort of overall structure that included all the Zuni towns, or perhaps only that the Spaniards *thought* so or wished to believe so.

Certain Pueblos outside of Zuni were willing to challenge the invaders. Some from Acoma, on its seemingly impregnable rock, killed several members of a Spanish party in December of 1598. Spanish reprisal was swift; the pueblo was overrun and 500 to 600 of its citizens were killed. Of the Indians captured, all males over the age of twenty-five were sentenced to have a foot cut off. All men and women over twelve, mutilated or not, were enslaved, and children were sent to various monasteries in New Spain. Two Hopi who were visiting Acoma had their right hands severed and were sent home as a warning in early 1599. That same year the Tompiro, unimpressed by the savage treatment of Acoma, also rebelled. They were beaten back with considerable losses. Two years later a second rebellion flared up in

that region and several hundred men, women, and children
were killed.

Because of the realities of travel in the roadless Southwest and the fact that Spanish control of the region centered
in the Rio Grande Valley, neither Zuni nor the even more
distant Hopi towns received much attention in the early
days of Spanish settlement. The Zuni leaders must have pon-
dered the Spanish brutality toward Acoma and the Tompiro
towns and weighed carefully their future course of action. It
was not until the summer of 1629 that a group of friars
reached Zuni and Hopi. This was an expedition in force, led
by the Spanish governor, Manuel de Silva Nieto, and the
Franciscan *custos* (custodian or head of the missions) of the
New Mexican missions, Father Estevan de Perea. The first
mission churches—La Purísima Concepción at Hawikuh,
the largest Zuni town at this time, and Nuestra Señora de
Guadalupe at Halona—were constructed in this period.
There were still six pueblos but only Hawikuh and Halona
were of any great demographic importance.

There was trouble almost from the first. In 1632, the
priest at Hawikuh, Francisco Letrado, was killed, and his
scalp was used ceremonially. A few days later a second
missionary, Martín de Arvide who was traveling south
from Zuni to the Sonoran area, was overtaken, killed, and
scalped by a Zuni war party. The Zuni were understandably
worried about the consequences of these actions and retreated to Dowa Yalanne. The Spaniards, now quite overex-
tended, either could not, or chose not to, attack in force.
The missionaries patched up a peace, but it would be another three years before the Zuni fully returned from the sacred mountain to their pueblos.

There apparently was no reestablishment of the Zuni

missions until some time in the period 1641–44. As the seventeenth century wore on, Halona gradually became the most important Zuni settlement. In the 1660s there was only one friar, Juan Galdo, who was stationed at Halona but who ministered to the church at Hawikuh as well as to a *visita* for each mother church at Matsak'ya and Kechibawa respectively. Visitas are temporary buildings in which masses are recited at weekly or monthly intervals. In 1672 two missionaries were at Zuni: Galdo at Halona and Father Pedro de Avila at Hawikuh. In that year Avila was murdered, presumably by Navajo or perhaps White Mountain Apache.

Throughout the seventeenth century the Pueblo Indian population of New Mexico and Arizona had been slowly declining. This was due partly to Spanish-introduced disease, partly to the economic, social, and religious disruption that followed Spanish rule, and partly to the fact that nomadic Indians, both Apache and Navajo, were pressing on the Pueblos. Outlying pueblos like Hawikuh were becoming dangerous places in which to live. In addition, Hawikuh, the entry port for the Sonoran and west Mexican trade, had lost much of its reason for being. Spain had overrun the northwest coast and northern mountains of Mexico, aided by European diseases that decimated the area. The Sonoran statelets, the lynchpins for the Mexican trade, had collapsed even before Jesuit missionaries pushed into the area, about the time when Zuni was receiving its first missionaries. In the Rio Grande Valley an estimated population of 50,000 in Coronado's time had dropped to 40,000 by the Oñate period. By the last decades of the seventeenth century it may have been near 15,000. Zuni and Hopi probably experienced a smaller percentage decline. If Zuni had as many as 3,000 to 3,500 people in Coronado's time, that number had shrunk somewhat by the Oñate entrada. Archaeologist Bertha P. Dutton, some years ago, suggested that in A.D. 1680 there were perhaps 2,500 individuals in the remaining Zuni towns. The population continued to decline during the eighteenth century, probably due mostly to a series of epidemic diseases including smallpox. A head count in the year 1776 listed 1,616 individuals. At the beginning of the American period, 1846, the population was about 1,200. Since that time the Zuni population has made a significant recovery. In 1881 the army officer John Burke estimated the number of Zuni at 1,700. The modern population is over 7,000.

The Zuni played a relatively minor role in the explosive revolt that shook the Pueblo world in 1680, though the friar at Halona, Juan de Bal, apparently the only missionary at Zuni that year, was slain. The Zuni people fled to Dowa Yalanne, but when Diego de Vargas reentered the Pueblo region in 1692 they gradually reoccupied Halona. All the other towns were deserted, at least as permanent settlements.

Zuni relations with the Spaniards continued minimal. As previously mentioned, they were visited in 1692 by de Vargas, who also made a tour of the Hopi towns. In 1696 a second revolt flared in the Rio Grande Valley and the Zuni cautiously maintained themselves on Dowa Yalanne. Then the Hopi made it clear that they intended to remain free of Spanish control by destroying the one pro-Spanish Hopi town, Awatobi. At Zuni, Father Juan de Garaycoechea rebuilt the mission of Nuestra Señora de Guadalupe at Halona. The new mission church probably utilized materials from the original church and seems to have been situated on its site.

Missionary activity at Zuni during the eighteenth century was limited. The Franciscans themselves did not consider the post to be a desirable one. Still, there were ambitious or visionary friars who dreamed of remissionizing the apostate Hopi, and Zuni was the nearest Franciscan operation to Hopi. One such visionary was Father Silvestre Vélez de Escalante, one of the leaders of the famous Domínguez-Escalante expedition of 1776, which explored large segments of the intermontane west. However, for the most part the Spanish presence in Zuni from the Pueblo Revolt onward had very little effect on the people and their social and religious life.

The period between the Pueblo Revolt and the coming of Americans saw the Zuni developing an extensive agriculture around the Zuni River and in its tributary valleys. They had already experimented with irrigation before the first Spanish *entradas,* and now they utilized both canal and floodwater irrigation to grow extensive crops of maize—as much as 10,000 acres according to early American accounts. Farming villages were established, some in the areas around sites deserted in the seventeenth century. In fact some stories suggest that Zuni summer farm camps may have been established as far west as the modern town of St. Johns on the Little Colorado River. By the 1860s, Zuni entrepreneurs were in a position to sell thousands of bushels of corn to the U.S. Army, which had established nearby Fort Defiance to control the Navajo. The Zuni also continued to hunt, as they had in aboriginal times, in the Zuni and San Francisco Valleys as well as in the Zuni and White Mountains. In addi-

tion, they sent small parties to the High Plains to hunt
bison, following a pattern that was already old when the
first Spaniards came.

Nor did the Zuni hesitate to incorporate European crops
into their economy. Melons had come in, probably with
Coronado. Oñate and his followers brought wheat and fruit
trees, especially peach trees, which were eagerly accepted
by the Zuni. Perhaps even more significant was the introduction of European animals. By the time of the Pueblo
Revolt, the Zuni had obtained horses, such animals being
documented in 1692 by de Vargas. Missionaries throughout
the Southwest had bred massive herds of sheep in the seventeenth century, having brought the hardy churro variety,
with its rough but serviceable wool, from central Spain.
Most or all of these sheep remained the property of the missions, but all over the Pueblo world natives were trained to
herd and care for them. As early as the seventeenth century,
the Navajo were building up their own sheep herds by raiding the Spanish missions and *estancias,* and after the Pueblo
Revolt the mission sheep fell into the hands of the various
Pueblos. By the early 1720s, herding was becoming well established at Zuni and by around 1759 sheep were estimated
to number 15,000 or more. A flourishing weaving industry
developed at the pueblo, and sheep became a favorite meat
animal. This brought Zuni to the attention of the neighbor-
ing nomads, the Navajo! Sheep and people stealing became a
favorite Navajo pastime at Zuni, as it was at Hopi. As Hopi
was completely outside and Zuni barely within the Spanish
military orbit, neither group could expect Spanish help. In
the Mexican period, which began with the independence of
Mexico around 1821, this was even more true because any
hope of missionization had been abandoned by that point.

During this long span of time (1680–1846), the Zuni honed their war skills probably more conscientiously than they had in prehistoric times. In the seventeenth century the Spaniards had enlisted Pueblo citizens as auxiliary soldiers and had encouraged the office of "Capitán de Guerra" and the taking of scalps—as long as they were Navajo or Apache. Now, with horses available, the Zuni held their own against the Navajo, though the outlying farming villages were never completely safe. Still, as in prehistoric times, there was trading as well as raiding, and Navajo often peacefully attended the great ceremonials, especially the winter solstice Shalako dances.

The arrival of the Americans in 1846 may have seemed at first sight to be somewhat to the advantage of the Zuni tribe. In the Treaty of Guadalupe Hidalgo signed with Mexico, the newcomers agreed to maintain the Spanish-Mexican land grants, including those given to the Indians. Exactly what the Spanish had granted to the Zuni was uncertain, the necessary documents having been lost—if they ever existed. A very limited "grant" from the Spanish crown was produced when reservations were being worked out, but that is now known to be a nineteenth-century forgery. Eventually a reservation that met minimal needs, though it failed to cover their historic use area, was assigned to the Zuni.

In addition, the Anglo-Americans had a vested interest in stopping the sporadic raiding of Zuni land by Navajo and Apache, and those sheep- and cattle-herding nomads very quickly felt pressure from U.S. military forces. This indirect military help plus the large purchases of Zuni grain by the American army made the pueblo more secure and introduced the beginnings of a money economy into Zuni. As we

will see below, the newcomers introduced other things as
well, not all of them to the Zunis' liking.

Interaction between the Anglo world and the Zuni began in earnest in the post – Civil War period. Aside from the army itself, several groups quickly impacted the Zuni. Perhaps the most intrusive was the Bureau of Indian Affairs, a branch of the federal government, charged with controlling and governing the various indigenous groups in the United States. Beginning in 1879 the first anthropologists arrived and certain of them eventually moved into the pueblo. The same was true of the traders, who, especially after about 1870, became active at Zuni and other pueblos. In this same period came a new wave of missionaries, this time primarily Protestant Christian rather than Catholic. A little later there was impingement on Zuni use lands by Anglo-American ranchers and, more ominously, land speculators.

An analysis of the impact of the Bureau of Indian Affairs on Zuni belongs to a broader study of formal governmental relationships with Native Americans, nationwide. There was relatively little on-the-ground presence of Indian agents at Zuni. The pueblo was governed by the Pueblo Agency centered at Santa Fe, which also overlooked the affairs of the Jicarilla Apache. The first agent visited Zuni in the year 1870, and Indian Service personnel traveled to Zuni only occasionally in subsequent years. Eventually the Pueblo Indian Agency established a subagency on the Zuni reservation, and to some degree it was drawn into the missionaries' fight to substitute an evangelical Christianity for the traditional Zuni religion.

On balance, the anthropologists were probably the most benign of the outside groups since, for the most part, they only wanted to study the Zuni, not to change them. However, even anthropologists in the nineteenth century were generally imbued with the racist attitudes of European society as a whole. At their best, they alerted the public to the grosser attempts at land grabs by speculators. At their worst, they were incredibly insensitive to the ceremonial culture of their long-suffering hosts. One of the earliest anthropologists, Frank Cushing of the Bureau of (American) Ethnology, attempted to learn Zuni and to function as participant-observer. Cushing served for a time as one of the bow priests, though it is not clear to what extent he really filled that complex office. He spoke some Zuni, but he was hardly fluent in the language. John Burke, who was at Zuni in 1881 was sympathetic and his information, though often naive, was reasonably correct for his time. Matilda Coxe Stevenson, who first visited Zuni in 1879, probably accumulated the most information about this pueblo. However, her methods of collecting information involved bullying techniques and downright deceit, leaving much to be desired. She is not well regarded in the pueblo today.

The traders, arriving in 1871, were also reasonably benign, although there was a considerable amount of variation in individual attitudes. As far as we know, as of 1870 no Zuni could speak English and very few knew any Spanish. By necessity, some of the traders and their children learned to speak Zuni, and they performed a considerable service in opening a window onto the world for the Zuni people. The earliest permanent trader was Douglas D. Graham, who moved to Zuni in 1878. More and more, Zuni individuals became interested in purchasing certain outside goods including metal cooking pots, guns and gunpowder, machine-made cheap cotton cloth, soap, condiments, sugar, and other foodstuffs.

As time went on, the traditional Zuni lands of the Southwest were nibbled away. The Navajo, who continued hostile to the Americans, were defeated by the army and forcibly resettled near Fort Sumner on the Pecos River of New Mexico in 1858. However, they were allowed to return to their old homelands in 1868 and soon began to expand from their reservation north of Gallup onto the eastern portion of the Zuni use area. Mormon farmers also impinged upon the region, as did Hispanic ranchers and herders. After the railroad was extended into western New Mexico in 1881, cattle companies and miners, too, pushed onto Zuni land. In 1877 President Rutherford B. Hayes established a Zuni use area running in a southwest to northeast direction from the Arizona border to just beyond the farming village of Pescado east of Dowa Yalanne. A competition quickly developed for the rich section of the Zuni drainage around Nutria, and it looked as if land speculators with powerful political interests in Washington, D.C., might wrest that region away from the Zuni. Fortunately, Frank Cushing, at the risk of his career in government service and with help from influential individuals in the East, was able to have the Nutria area declared part of the reservation in 1883. In the past century, the reservation has been extended by acts of Congress. It now totals a little over 400,000 acres (636 square miles).

Of all the influences upon the Zuni, that of the missionaries was perhaps the most controversial. Missionaries in all the late-nineteenth-century European colonial powers routinely confused the contemporary values of western society with religion. The vast majority of missionaries believed firmly in the racial and cultural superiority of Europeans, and normally did not hesitate to further European imperial interests. Their religions were generally of a simplistic, evangelical type, differing in technical detail (Catholic from Protestant, Baptist from Presbyterian, etc.) but employing much the same means for the same ends. In the United States during this period, as far as Indians were concerned, the ends were to turn the various Native American groups into acceptable, even though racially second-class, Americans. The means generally were the destruction of native language, religion, and culture.

The missionaries at Zuni were neither the best nor the worst examples of their type. They arrived at a time when the Bureau of Indian Affairs had given over many of the Indian Service duties to missionaries, usually Protestant. Ignoring separation of church and state, the federal government supplied funds for schools, and the missionaries ran them often with little or no supervision.

In 1876 an attempt by Mormon missionaries to convert the Zuni led to over a hundred baptisms. The following year a Mormon settlement was founded at Ramah, near the eastern edge of the Zuni reservation. This seems to have spurred personnel of the Pueblo Agency, who leaned to Presbyterianism, to take some action. In 1878 an early missionary, Taylor F. Ealy, with his wife and two daughters, arrived to set up a Presbyterian mission and take over the school at Zuni, which had begun the previous year. With them was an assistant teacher, Jennie Hammaker. Neither the school nor the mission was particularly successful—not too puzzling since the Zuni did not speak English and the Ealy family lacked competence in the Zuni language. There was also tension between the Presbyterians and the Mormons, the latter group continuing to harbor ambitions in the Zuni missionary field. Anthropologists like Frank Cush-

ing and John G. Bourke seem to have disliked the missionaries, though all sides agreed that the Zuni should receive a
western education.

Mary E. DeSette, who arrived in 1889, brought more
ruthless attempts at acculturation. At boarding schools in
this period, use of native speech was forbidden, and children were harshly punished for lapsing into their own languages. It was probably impossible to have such complete
linguistic control at the day-school arrangement at Zuni, but
DeSette, backed by the Pueblo Agency and to some degree
by the army, did her best to promote rapid and ruthless
acculturation. However, she quickly became embroiled in
a witch controversy, and her sexual bigotry aimed at the be-
loved *lhamana* or *berdache* (cross dresser), We'wha, was not
popular at Zuni. Her brutal teaching methods eventually
caused a reaction and, in any case, the U.S. government
ended its subsidy of mission schools in the year 1897. In the
government day school that was opened that year, DeSette
had no place. She stayed on in Zuni for a time, and through
the winter of 1889–99 she became somewhat of a heroine
by helping to fight a smallpox epidemic that killed several
hundred Zuni. In 1899 she was quietly transferred.

Tensions at Zuni finally persuaded the Indian Service to
establish a subagency at Black Rock on the Zuni Reservation. In 1907 a boarding school was opened there, while
another mission school, under the auspices of the Dutch
Reformed Church, was set up in 1908. In 1921 the Franciscans, absent from the area since the early nineteenth century, founded St. Anthony's, a new mission. Two years later
they began a mission school. Of all the modern missionaries, the Franciscans seem to be the most attuned to the Zuni
lifeways. Perhaps the most telling, certainly the most vis-

ual, example of this is the rejuvenation of the ancient Zuni mission church, with dramatic paintings of the Zuni summer and winter ceremonial rounds on the opposite walls of the nave.

The twentieth century saw a changing world. At first, church and state continued to press their own agendas upon the Zuni people. However, as the century wore on, the outside world began to develop an increasing awareness of the cultural values that Zuni and other Native Americans could bring to the nation. Missionary voices were muted, and the Bureau of Indian Affairs began to tread more softly. A series of court decisions at the national level increasingly guaranteed Native Americas, the Zuni among them, basic rights, not necessarily as Indians, but as American citizens.

At Virgil Wyaco's birth this awareness was in its infancy. It is stronger now and its strength will surely continue to grow. In the twenty-first century, it may be that Virgil's grandchildren's grandchildren will see a new Zuni, an integral part of the national life, but with a Zuni culture paralleling that life and transcending it.

SUGGESTED READINGS

Anyon, Roger

1992   The late Prehistoric and Early Historic Periods in
the Zuni–Cibola Area, A.D. 1400–1680. In *Current
Research on the Late Prehistory and Early History of New
Mexico,* ed. B. J. Vierra and C. Gualtieri. Albuquerque:
New Mexico Archaeological Council, Special Publication
1, 75–83.

Crampton, C. Gregory

1977   *The Zuni of Cibola.* Salt Lake City: University of
Utah Press.

Dutton, Bertha P.

1963a   *Friendly People: The Zuni Indians.* Santa Fe:
Museum of New Mexico Press.

1963b   *Sun Father's Way.* Albuquerque: University of
New Mexico Press.

1975   *American Indians of the Southwest.* Albuquerque:
University of New Mexico Press

Eggan, Fred, and T. N. Pandey

1979   Zuni History, 1850–1970. In *Handbook of North
American Indians*, Vol. 9: *Southwest,* ed. A. Ortiz.
Washington, D.C.: Smithsonian Institution, 474–89.

Ferguson, T. J., and E. Richard Hart

1985   *A Zuni Atlas.* Norman: University of Oklahoma
Press.

144 / Ferguson, T. J., and Barbara Mills

    1982   *Archaeological Investigations at Zuni Pueblo, New Mexico, 1977–1980.* Zuni Archaeological Program, Report 183.

Green, Jesse

    1979   *Selected Writings of Frank Hamilton Cushing.* Lincoln: University of Nebraska Press.

Kintigh, Keith W.

    1990   Protohistoric Transitions in the Western Pueblo Area. In *Perspectives on Southwestern Prehistory,* ed. P. E. Minnis and C. L. Redman. Boulder: Westview Press.

Ladd, Edmund J.

    1979a   Zuni Social and Political Organization. In *Handbook of North American Indians,* Vol. 9: *Southwest,* ed. A. Ortiz. Washington, D.C.: Smithsonian Institution, 482–91.

    1979b   Zuni Economy. In *Handbook of North American Indians,* Vol. 9: *Southwest,* ed. A. Ortiz. Washington, D.C.: Smithsonian Institution, 492–98.

    1994   Cushing among the Zuñi—A Zuñi Perspective. *Gilcrease Journal* 2 (Autumn): 20–35.

Riley, Carroll L.

    1975   The Road to Hawikuh: Trade and Trade Routes to Cíbola-Zuni. *The Kiva* 41: 137–59.

    1987   *The Frontier People.* Albuquerque: University of New Mexico Press.

    1995   *Rio del Norte.* Salt Lake City: University of Utah Press.

Roscoe, Will

    1991   *The Zuni Man-Woman.* Albuquerque: University of New Mexico Press.

Schaafsma, Polly
 1992   *Rock Art in New Mexico.* Santa Fe: Museum of New
 Mexico Press.
Stevenson, Matilda Coxe
 1904   *The Zuñi Indians.* Twenty-Third Annual Report of
 the Bureau of American Ethnology, 1901–02.
 Washington, D.C.: Bureau of American Ethnology.
Tedlock, Dennis
 1979   Zuni Religion and World View. In *Handbook of
 North American Indians,* Vol. 9: *Southwest,* ed. A. Ortiz.
 Washington, D.C.: Smithsonian Institution, 499–508.
Woodbury, Richard B.
 1979   Zuni Prehistory and History to 1850. In
 Handbook of North American Indians, Vol. 9: *Southwest,* ed.
 A. Ortiz. Washington, D.C.: Smithsonian Institution,
 467–73.